CLASSIC EPHEMERA

CLASSIC *f*M

Classic Ephemera

A classical music omnibus

compiled by

Darren Henley & Tim Lihoreau

BOOSEY&HAWKES

Published by Boosey & Hawkes Music Publishers Ltd
Aldwych House
71–91 Aldwych
London
WC2B 4HN

in association with Classic FM
7 Swallow Place
Oxford Circus
London
W1B 2AG

www.boosey.com
www.classicfm.com

© Copyright 2005 by Darren Henley and Tim Lihoreau

ISBN 0-81562-467-7

Cover illustration by Sally Kindberg. Cover design by Design United Digital Ltd.

First impression 2005

Printed in England by Halstan & Co Ltd, Amersham, Bucks

Contents

About the authors

Darren Henley is the Station Manager of Classic FM. His radio programmes have been honoured by the Sony Radio Academy Awards, the British Radio Awards, the New York International Radio Festival and the United Nations. He writes regularly for Classic FM Magazine. Previously, a journalist for ITN and Invicta Radio in Kent, he is the co-author of *Aled: The Autobiography* (with Aled Jones) published by Virgin Books and of two audiobooks for children – one of which, *The Story of Classical Music*, was nominated for a Grammy Award in 2005.

Tim Lihoreau is the Creative Director of Classic FM. He studied music at the University of Leeds and worked as a professional pianist before joining Jazz FM, from where he moved to Classic FM. He has been responsible for writing and producing many of the station's most acclaimed programmes, which have been honoured by the Sony Radio Academy Awards, the NTL Commercial Radio Awards and the New York International Radio Festival. His books include *Stephen Fry's Incomplete and Utter History of Classical Music* published by Boxtree.

Introduction

Classic FM has always believed that classical music should be a part of everyone's life. If you already listen to the music we play every day and you want to know more about it, then you've come to the right place.

This may not be the biggest book about classical music that you'll be able to find. But what it lacks in size, it makes up for in facts, stories and, most important of all, recommendations for great music to listen to.

As we put together our radio programmes, we often discover fascinating facts and titillating titbits about the world of classical music. After many years of collecting this information, we've decided to gather it all together for the first time in one single book, which spans composer biographies, instrument profiles, general trivia, lengthy lists and quotable sayings. This is the result.

So if you're hoping to uncover the killer fact to spice up your after-dinner conversation; if you want to dazzle your friends with your knowledge of the stories behind the greatest classical music; or if, like us, you're simply an acquirer of trivia, we hope there will be something for you in the next one hundred and fifty or so pages.

If you haven't listened to Classic FM yet, then hopefully this book will well and truly whet your appetite, as well as answering some of the questions about classical music that you've always wanted to ask.

Darren Henley
Tim Lihoreau

Classical music terms

CHAMBER MUSIC

So called because it was written for groups small enough to play in the privacy of their own chamber, or room. Replaced nowadays by the Sony PlayStation 2. Chamber music can be for anything from a couple of soloists to larger chamber orchestras, which usually have up to 30 or so players. That's compared with a full symphony orchestra, which can have as many as 80 to 100 performers on the stage at any one time.

Check it out Schubert: *The Trout* | Mozart: *Clarinet Quintet* |
Mendelssohn: *Octet*

★ ★ ★

CHRISTMAS MUSIC

The tunes of some of the best-loved carols were, in fact, written by classical music greats (*Hark the Herald* by Mendelssohn, *See amid the winter's snow* by Holst). As well as the hymns we sing each year, there's also a festive sack-load of longer pieces, such as the *Carol Symphony* by the exquisitely named Victor Hely-Hutchinson, which are perfect for having on in the background as the family arrive on Christmas Eve.

★ ★ ★

CONCERTO

A piece of music, usually in three movements, written for a solo instrument accompanied by an orchestra. When a concerto is performed, the soloist, who is very much the star of the show, usually stands or sits at the front of the stage next to the conductor. Incidentally, in music, a **movement** does not refer to the stampede towards the bar at the interval of a concert. Instead, it is one section of a bigger piece. Usually, different movements are played at different speeds, indicated by those Italian instructions of which composers are so fond.

Check it out

Vivaldi: *Four Seasons* | Mozart: Piano Concerto No. 21 | Mendelssohn: Violin Concerto in E minor | Rachmaninoff: Piano Concerto No. 2

★ ★ ★

ERAS

Any music that was composed before 1600 is said to be from the *early* period. Gregorian chant falls into this category (named after Pope Gregory who did much to develop church music), lots of which is very beautiful and relaxing.

Music written between, roughly, 1600 and 1750 is described as coming from the *baroque* period. Composers who were producing new material at this time include Bach, Handel and Vivaldi.

Now, here's a funny one. Everything we play on Classic FM is classical music. But anything written between roughly 1750 and 1830 is described as coming from the *classical* period. This includes the work of Haydn and Mozart. Beethoven, too, wrote some music in the classical period but he also stayed on after the bell had gone for the early romantic period and wrote some stuff in that one too.

Love features heavily in classical music, just as it does in pop. But, when we are talking about eras, *romantic* refers to the composers who were writing music from roughly 1830 to 1900, including Schubert, Chopin and Berlioz.

Modern music is another odd one. Anything written after 1900 is generally referred to as coming from the *modern* period, despite the fact that some of it is now over a hundred years old. A car of equivalent age would be vintage. In time, we may come to call it twentieth-century music, to allow for stuff written after the year 2000.

If you imagine that eras in music are like star signs, with *modern* as Aquarius (genius or mad, hard to tell), *romantic* as Cancer (slushy, doe-eyed, dreamy) and *classical* as Gemini (sometimes slushy, sometimes not), then *baroque* is clearly the Virgo – neat, tidy, everything in its place, but never too much emotion.

FILM MUSIC

There's a long history of music being used in films, right back to the days when a pianist would accompany silent movies with a live performance. Many of the greatest pieces of classical music by composers as varied as Mozart, Beethoven and Wagner have been used in films. Add to this a long tradition of composers being commissioned to write music especially for the cinema and we're talking quite a large section in the record shop. Copland, Vaughan Williams, Walton, Prokofieff and Shostakovich all have soundtracks to their names. More recently, Howard Shore, John Barry, James Horner and Hans Zimmer have all given the undoubted king of movie composers, John Williams, a run for his money. The first-ever dedicated soundtrack was composed by Saint-Saëns for the 1908 film *L'assassinat du Duc de Guise*.

INCIDENTAL MUSIC

Stretching back to ancient Greek times, incidental music is the forerunner to the film soundtrack. As in Grieg's music to Ibsen's play *Peer Gynt*, it was often written to add atmosphere to the action on stage or even to fill in the sections where the director thought 'What shall we do in this bit where nothing's going on?' If nothing else, incidental music lets the audience know that now is really not the time to nip out for a choc-ice.

Check it out

Mendelssohn: incidental music to *A Midsummer Night's Dream* | Sibelius: *Karelia Suite*, which started life as incidental music to a student play | Bizet: incidental music to Daudet's play *L'Arlésienne*

★ ★ ★

INSTRUCTIONS

The Italian word *adagio* is a composer's way of telling a performer to play their music very slowly. It is slower than andante but faster than largo. Slow movements, in general are often simply called 'adagios' because so many bear this marking.

At the other end of the scale, *allegro* is another instruction from a composer to a performer. The message is to play fast – not, however, as fast as *presto* but faster than *allegretto* (which means allegro-ish). Probably the most famous allegro of all is the 'da da da DER…' of Beethoven's 5th Symphony.

Allegro is not to be confused with Allegri or the Austin Allegro. The first is a composer born in the 16th century, best known for his choral masterpiece *Miserere*. The second is a 1970s car often favoured by aunties and geography teachers. Paradoxically neither of these groups is exactly renowned for being fast.

Legato is another order composers like to issue to musicians – this time they are asking the performer to play smoothly. The opposite is *staccato* – a rather spikier sound.

So why are all these instructions in Italian? Well, Italy was once the centre of the music industry and therefore all the composers wrote their directions in Italian. This continues today, meaning that a German composer writing for a Spanish pianist and a Dutch violinist would still tell them what speed to play in Italian. Odd, but true.

INTERMEZZO

This is the operatic equivalent of your TV screen going all soft focus and a caption reading 'Ten Years Later' appearing. Don't you just hate it when that happens? Well, an intermezzo – which is the Italian word for 'the bit stuck in' – is a piece of orchestral music in the middle of an opera, which is used to show the audience that a period of time has gone by. But, oddly enough, it's nowhere near as annoying as a 'Ten Years Later' caption.

NOCTURNE

Written for the piano, these short pieces were invented by the Irish composer John Field. Chopin then developed the idea further. They are perfect to listen to as a late evening wind-down, as they are intended to suggest the calm of the night.

Namedrop Chopin: *Nocturne in A Flat* and Debussy: *Nocturnes* for Orchestra, decidedly different yet equally rewarding pieces.

OPERA

Operas tend to be big on great tunes, passion, sorrow, romance and drama. Sadly, they are rarely big on plot. Opera storylines tend to centre around either unrequited love, or bizarre 'what do you mean you're really a horse in disguise' madness. Broadly speaking though, most opera storylines go something like this: Man falls in love with woman. Woman turns out to be either related or someone she claimed not to be. Man and woman's love domed. Cue angst (in song). Woman (can be man – doesn't matter) dies horrific death, preferably involving consumption. Remaining lover dies. Big song. End. Everyone goes down the pub. In fact, opera is really what classical music would be like if Quentin Tarantino had invented it. But despite the high body count, it has given us some of the most spectacular and beautiful pieces anywhere in classical music. For ten famous potted opera plots in detail, turn to page 77.

OPUS

The Latin word for 'work', used, simply, to put together a database of a composer's work in chronological order. So Opus 3 would be the third piece that a composer had written. Opus numbers tend to follow the published date of a work, not necessarily the date the composer wrote it. Hence, Chopin's published *Piano Concertos* 1 and 2 were actually written in the order 2 and 1 (see page 30). Mozart and J S Bach have their own numbering systems. Mozart's was done by Ludwig von Köchel, who, being a shy and retiring sort of chap, decided to give each of Mozart's works a Köchel number instead of an Opus number. In J S Bach's case, his pieces all have BWV in front of the number. These initials stand for *Bachs Werke-Verzeichnis*, which is German for 'Catalogue of Bach's Works', and are not, as some think, a 'best before' date mark.

Namedrop Three great numbers to learn are: Beethoven's Opus 67, Mozart's K622, and Tchaikovsky's Opus 20 – great to drop in at parties. (They are Beethoven's *Fifth Symphony*, Mozart's *Clarinet Concerto* and Tchaikovsky's *Swan Lake*.)

ORATORIO

Often staged in a church or cathedral, an oratorio is a religious story set to music and performed by solo singers, a choir and an orchestra. Usually though, the story is told without scenery and costumes – so the event is more of a concert. In the end, it's a bit like opera, only cheaper. Probably the most famous oratorio is *Messiah* by Handel.

Check it out

Mendelssohn: *Elijah* | Walton: *Belshazzar's Feast* | and if you're feeling up to a choral bath, Elgar: *The Dream of Gerontius*

★ ★ ★

OVERTURE

There are two types of overture. Type A – the bit that comes at the beginning of an opera. It's very often a sort of greatest hits showcase of the tunes that will follow. Sometimes, though, composers will write an overture that doesn't have anything else coming afterwards (Type B). Possibly the most famous example of this is Tchaikovsky's *1812 Overture*.

Check it out

The overture to Mozart's *The Marriage of Figaro* (A) | Tchaikovsky's fantasy overture *Romeo and Juliet* (B) | Wagner's overture to *The Flying Dutchman* (A) | Brahms' *Academic Festival Overture* (B)

★ ★ ★

SINGERS

Sopranos are the highest female voices, providing not only the female lead but also, more often than not, the love-interest for the male tenors in opera. Sopranos often heard on Classic FM include Maria Callas, Renée Fleming, Lesley Garrett and Angela Gheorghiù. Mezzo-sopranos, such as Cecilia Bartoli, have voices that are slightly deeper.

Altos are usually female singers who either can't sing as high as sopranos, or who can but want a quiet life, free from throat strain. Just as violas are the slightly lower, some would say duller, versions of violins, so the altos are …

well, let's leave it there, shall we? Men can be altos too, but … well, again, let's just leave it there.

Tenors are generally the 'heroes' of the opera world, getting many of the best male arias. The most well-known are The Three Tenors – Luciano Pavarotti, José Carreras and Placido Domingo – a trio who have become multi-millionaires on the back of their stadium concerts around the globe.

Baritones are male singers whose voices are higher than basses, but lower than tenors. So if you can't reach the high notes and have only ever been able to get the low notes first thing in the morning, best become a baritone. The international superstar Bryn Terfel is a fine example of a **bass-baritone**, whose voices, predictably, lie somewhere between basses and baritones.

The **basses** are the lowest of the male singers, the ones who sound like they've just got up after a heavy night on the sauce. In opera, they don't get as many of the hero roles as the tenors: if this seems unfair, listen to Lee Marvin singing in *Paint your Wagon* and ask yourself – would you elope with him? Incidentally, bass is pronounced 'base'. Again, quite apt if you remember Lee Marvin's character.

The girls aren't the only ones who can sing high in classical music. **Counter-tenors**, such as James Bowman or Andreas Scholl, have voices that are higher than tenors. However, they hit the high notes without having had to resort to surgery. This was not the case with **castrati**, who were castrated to ensure that their voices never broke. The practice was worryingly fashionable in the 18th century, with castrati even being resident in the Vatican. Alessandro Moreschi, who died in 1922, was the last known castrato and became rather famous in the process. He was the director of the Sistine Chapel Choir in Rome. Nowadays, we're all for loving music, but castration really is a snip too far.

If you hear somebody talking about a singer, no matter what type their voice, or whether they are male or female, performing an *aria*, this basically means they are singing a 'song'. Most of the big hits from operas are arias. They are the solos or set pieces performed by singers playing the big roles.

SONATA

A piece of music usually written either for a solo instrument, or for any single instrument with a piano. It's written in three or four movements and follows a set of rules so complicated it would make the Civil Service jealous.

SYMPHONY

This is a large-scale piece, normally written for an orchestra. It usually has four separate moments, and was once considered the greatest challenge to which a composer could aspire. Like buses, they rarely come in ones. Having said that, unlike buses, they seem to come in nines – Beethoven, Schubert and Mahler each wrote nine of them.

Check it out

Ten great symphonies
Beethoven: 9th (*Choral*) | Mozart: 40th | Brahms: 3rd | Dvořák: 9th (*New World*) | Haydn: 94th (*Surprise*) | Berlioz: *Symphonie fantastique* | Mahler: 5th | Tchaikovsky: 5th | Shostakovich: 5th | Schubert: 8th (*Unfinished*)

The instruments of the orchestra

Imagine. Four different types of instruments – some thirty string players alone, as well as ten or so brass, around the same number of woodwind and a liberal sprinkling of percussionists. Seventy-odd different players in all, spread out over a space the size of a tennis court, being told what to do by a guy (or girl) who might never have played a note in his (or her) life. Shouldn't work, should it? But it does. Amazingly.

The human windmill waving the stick in front of the orchestra is the conductor. A passable conductor can be the difference between a bad and a good performance. A great conductor can be the difference between a good and an unforgettable one. (Every now and again in the papers, you will see reviews of concerts where a 'golden silence' occurred at the end of a work, when everyone was just too overwhelmed to start clapping.) If you can't quite work out exactly what it is conductors do, imagine them in the same category as those new tights for women which support the bottom – without them, things tend to go pear-shaped.

This is how orchestras are conventionally set out on stage, although conductors are free to indulge in a game of musical chairs and move everyone around if they so wish.

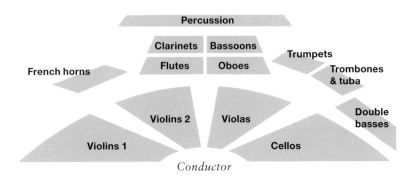

BASSOON

The bassoon is the lowest woodwind instrument of the orchestra. It looks something like a digeridoo wearing too much jewellery, but with an espresso frother coming out of the side. In fact, just like espresso, it too comes in single and double varieties.

Check it out Boccherini: *Bassoon Concerto* | Mozart: *Bassoon Concerto* | The theme from the children's television programme *Ivor the Engine*

Namedrop Best not let on you know any bassoonists

★ ★ ★

CELLO

This string instrument, played between the knees, comes between the viola and double bass in terms of pitch. It's more or less an oversized violin, although you shouldn't try getting one under your chin as the spike would certainly smart a bit. If you imagine the violin, viola, cello and double bass as being roughly the string equivalent of soprano, alto, tenor and bass, respectively, then the cello is the heroic, hunky tenor.

Check it out Elgar: *Cello Concerto* | Bach: *Cello Suites*

Namedrop Mstislav Rostropovich | Jacqueline du Pré | Julian Lloyd Webber | Steven Isserlis | Yo-Yo Ma

★ ★ ★

CLARINET

This is the most mellow of the woodwind instruments in the orchestra. When jazz and classical music meet, there's often a clarinet to be found somewhere towards the front of things. A modern clarinet has around 20 keys. Spare a thought for a clarinet player at the time when Mozart wrote his clarinet concerto. Back then, the clarinet had just six keys. The clarinettist had to play all the same notes a player does today, but with 14 fewer keys.

Check it out
Mozart: *Clarinet Concerto* | Copland: *Clarinet Concerto* | the start of the 2nd movement of Rachmaninoff's *Symphony No. 2* | Gershwin: *Rhapsody in Blue*

Namedrop
The late Jack Brymer became famous as the LSO's principal clarinettist from 1971 until his retirement.

★ ★ ★

COR ANGLAIS

The cor anglais, which translates as 'English horn', is one of the less well-known instruments of the orchestra. Many people mistakenly think that it must be part of the brass section. It actually looks like an over-sized oboe and resides firmly in the family of woodwind instruments. Anybody who says they can tell it apart from an oboe is either (a) a genius, (b) a liar, or (c) a cor anglais player.

Check it out
You can hear the cor anglais playing the main tune in the slow movement of Dvořák's *New World Symphony* and playing the part of the swan in *The Swan of Tuonela* by Sibelius

Namedrop
As with bassoonists, it's not recommended that you actually name any cor anglais players. If you are ever asked to provide details, simply adopt a misty-eyed, far-away look and sigh, knowingly.

★ ★ ★

DOUBLE BASS

Only the harp rivals this giant as the most difficult orchestral instrument to fit in the back of an estate car. Composers often use the deep sound of the double bass not just for its low, sonorous effect but also to add a little light relief to their music. For example, in Saint-Saëns' *Carnival of the Animals*, it plays the part of the elephant – another thing that it's difficult to get in the back of an estate car.

Check it out

Double Bass Concerto by Karl Ditters von Dittersdorf. Crazy name, crazy guy.

Well I never!

Serge Koussevitsky, legendary conductor with the Boston Symphony Orchestra, was a virtuoso double bass player.

★ ★ ★

FLUTE

This is at the smaller end of the woodwind family. It's still classed as woodwind even though it's usually made from metal. Among the flute's good points, it's perfect for kids to take up, being small enough to be carried to school. Among the bad points, it's very easy to leave on the bus.

Check it out

Mozart: *Flute Concerto* | Fauré: *Pavane*

Namedrop

Sir James Galway is one of those classical musicians who successfully crossed over into a pop star level of fame during the 1970s and 1980s, not least because of the colour of his instrument. Rather than mere silver, he was known as 'the man with the golden flute'. James Bond, eat your heart out.

★ ★ ★

FRENCH HORN

A member of the brass family, if this instrument is uncoiled it would not only stretch for more than three metres, it would also give you something to do on a Sunday afternoon. Best not attempted during the quiet bit in a concert, though. Great composers for the horn include Mozart and Richard Strauss.

Check it out

Mozart: five *Horn Concertos* | Weber: *Concertino for Horn* | Richard Strauss: *Horn Concerto* – possibly for the more adventurous (his father was a horn player in Wagner's orchestra).

Namedrop

The greatest horn player in living memory is widely acknowledged to be Dennis Brain, who was killed in a car crash in 1957 at the tragically young age of 36.

★ ★ ★

GUITAR

The guitar in classical music is not quite the macho, trendy 'axe' of its rock music cousin. In fact, next to the full orchestra it has to fight to be heard, and is more often found in smaller groups or played solo. That's not to say there aren't some great guitar and orchestra pieces.

Check it out

Rodrigo: *Concierto de Aranjuez* | Tarrega: *Recuerdos de l'Alhambra* – both works which evoke warm Spanish countryside

Namedrop

Julian Bream | John Williams

★ ★ ★

HARP

It may make a heavenly noise but carrying it is a hell of a job. One of the hardest orchestral instruments to play, the harp nevertheless makes a beautiful sound. When harpists run their fingers all the way across the strings, creating that amazing, dream-like sound, it's called a 'glissando'.

Check it out
Mozart: *Flute and Harp Concerto*

Namedrop
The Prince of Wales has recently rekindled the tradition of appointing a harpist to his court. The first of these was Catrin Finch and the second Jemimah Philips

Well I never!
One of Beethoven's string quartets is nicknamed the *Harp Quartet* because Ludwig wrote glissandos (see above) shared between all four players.

Not to be confused with: Harmonica (mouth organ) players often refer to their instruments as the 'harp'. Don't muddle the two types of harp – it could hurt. While we're on the subject of the harmonica, did you know that every child in Belgium is required by law to take up the instrument while they are at school?

★ ★ ★

OBOE

A black, wooden instrument that looks a bit like a clarinet with a straw sticking out of the top. It has a more 'nasal' sound than the clarinet, but, played well, can sound utterly beautiful. Played badly, it can bring to mind Sweep from 'The Sooty Show' being attacked by geese. Either way, its piercing sound can always be heard through everything else. It's also the instrument you hear before an orchestral concert, playing the note to which all other instruments tune.

Check it out

Albinoni: *Oboe Concerto* | Ravel: *Boléro* | Jean Françaix: *The Flower Clock*

Namedrop

A bit like bassoon, this one – nobody will ever chastise you for not knowing names of oboe players. Maybe keep composer and oboe player Heinz Holliger in reserve, for special occasions.

Well I never!

A Heckelphone is the name given to the now largely obsolete baritone oboe, invented in 1904 by, not surprisingly, a Mr Heckel.

★ ★ ★

ORGAN

Known as 'The King of Instruments', these mighty beasts demand that orchestras and audiences come to them. Many organ performances take place in cathedrals or churches, although there are some concert halls with permanent built-in organs. The organ is played not only with the hands, but also the feet, which get their own 'shoe-sized' keyboard under the main organ.

Check it out

J S Bach: *Toccata and Fugue* in D minor | Widor: *Organ Symphony* No. 5 | Saint-Saëns: *Organ Symphony*

★ ★ ★

PERCUSSION

Orchestral instruments that you either hit or shake. They include the timpani (or kettledrums), cymbals, glockenspiel, xylophone, marimba, triangle, tambourine, castanets, tubular bells, side drum and bass drum. The percussion section also provides some of the more unusual sound effects that a composer can ask for, such as car horns, wind machines and car suspension springs.

Triangle in Liszt's *Piano Concerto* No. 1 | Tubular bells in Tchaikovsky's *1812 Overture* | Castanets in Manuel de Falla's *The Three-Cornered Hat*

Namedrop

Evelyn Glennie | Colin Currie

★ ★ ★

PIANO

Invented in Florence, around 1709, modern-day pianos come in many shapes and sizes. 'Piano' is short for 'pianoforte', which is the Italian for 'quiet loud'. It's one of the few instruments that can play lots of notes at once – so virtually every composer wrote some great stuff for the piano.

The list of composers who have written big piano hits is virtually endless: Chopin, Schumann, Field, Liszt, Mozart, Beethoven and Rachmaninoff to name but a few.

Namedrop

Evgeny Kissin | Martha Argerich | Maria João Pires | Freddy Kempf

★ ★ ★

SAXOPHONE

As musical instruments go, the saxophone is one of the new kids on the block. It was invented by a Belgian called Adolphe Sax around 1840. Even though saxophones are made of brass, they sit in the woodwind section of the orchestra because they're similar to play to the clarinet. Without a doubt, they occupy a special position as the coolest of the wind instruments.

Check it out

Debussy, Vaughan Williams, Berlioz, Bizet and Glazounoff have all written pieces featuring the sax. Their popularity has been somewhat overshadowed recently by *Parce mihi Domine* from the album *Officium*, a collaboration between the jazz saxophonist Jan Garbarek and the early music vocal group, The Hilliard Ensemble. The sound that they create is crossover music at its very best.

Namedrop

British sax player John Harle

TROMBONE

The sliding metal tube on a trombone not only lengthens or shortens the pipework to give the instrument a different pitch, it also gives it its 'comedy' value, providing that somewhat *Carry On ...* sound. They are the powerhouses of the brass section of the orchestra.

Check it out

The trombone was first used in a symphony by Beethoven in his Symphony No. 5

Namedrop

Ian Bousefield (principal trombone with the Vienna Philharmonic Orchestra) | Christian Lindberg

★ ★ ★

TRUMPET

This is the best-known member of the brass family, with a long history stretching back to biblical times. It is more agile than the trombone because it has three buttons (valves) instead of a slide. Its ability to be heard over a church organ has made it very popular at weddings.

Check it out

Hummel: *Trumpet Concerto* | John Stanley: *Trumpet Voluntary in D* | Haydn: *Trumpet Concerto* | Armenian composer Arutiunian's *Trumpet Concerto*, an absolute staple of the trumpet player's repertoire.

Namedrop

Wynton Marsalis | John Wallace | Håkan Hardenberger

TUBA

They're big, they're bold and they're brassy. But enough about tuba players. This enormous instrument tends not to be the star of the show, instead operating in a 'Best Supporting' role.

Check it out

Vaughan Williams: *Tuba Concerto* – one of the few occasions when the tuba takes centre stage

Namedrop

Khachaturian (*see composers section*) | Other than that, you can get away with namedropping Tubby.

★ ★ ★

VIOLA

Often the butt of jokes among professional musicians, the viola looks just like a violin, but is slightly bigger, makes a deeper sound and burns for longer when you set fire to it. That's the punchline to one of the jokes, by the way.

Check it out

William Walton: *Viola Concerto*

Namedrop

Best spare their embarrassment, really.

★ ★ ★

VIOLIN

There is safety in numbers if you are a violin player in an orchestra: around twenty to thirty other people sitting next to you playing the same instrument, all following the leader (the one at the front, nearest the conductor).

Check it out

Another one of those instruments which has been well serviced by a plethora of composers over the years with big concertos from Mozart, Beethoven, Brahms, Bruch, Mendelssohn and Tchaikovsky. Paganini was an amazing fiddler himself and left pieces which are still touchstones in virtuosity today.

Namedrop

Itzhak Perlman | Yehudi Menuhin | Nigel Kennedy | Anne-Sophie Mutter | Maxim Vengerov | Joshua Bell

★ ★ ★

The great composers

Tomaso ALBINONI (1671–1751)

Best known for his *Adagio* for Organ and Strings, even though it was actually written by an Italian professor in 1958 – the same year as Pele scored a hat-trick in the World Cup in Sweden. It was based on only a fragment of the original manuscript. So, Albinoni wrote hundreds of tunes in his lifetime but is now famous for one he didn't write. A bit like jazz musician, Dave Brubeck, and his hit *Take Five*.

Check it out
Oboe Concerto No. 2

Namedrop
Remo Giazotto, the Italian professor who reworked the *Adagio*.

★ ★ ★

Sir Malcolm ARNOLD (born 1921)

Arnold gave up his job as principal trumpet in the London Philharmonic Orchestra to become a full-time composer. He became particularly well-known through his work for the cinema and won an Oscar for his soundtrack to *The Bridge on the River Kwai*.

Check it out
Eight English Dances | Four Scottish Dances | Four Cornish Dances

★ ★ ★

Johann Sebastian BACH (1685–1750)

This German composer was the most famous of a large musical family. Alongside Handel, he was one of he greatest composers of the baroque period. He was also an organist and church music master, which is why lots of his stuff is religious.

When he was only 19, he walked from his home in Arnstadt to Lübeck to hear a performance by his favourite composer, Buxtehude. The teenager then walked all the way back to Arnstadt, a total journey of some 420 miles.

If Bach's *Goldberg Variations* sends you to sleep, don't worry. That's what the composer intended. Bach wrote the keyboard work for one Count Kayserling, an insomniac at the Dresden court, who commissioned him to come up with something 'soft and yet a little gay' to help him sleep. The count's musicians were given the job of playing all 30 variations to him at night. Bach is also noted for writing *Wachet auf*, which translates as 'Sleepers Awake'.

One of Bach's most famous pieces, his *Air on the G string*, wasn't so called by the composer himself. In fact, it wasn't written to be played on a G string at all. It got this nickname when a 19th-century fiddler called August Wilhelmj rearranged it as a bit of a novelty.

The Bach dynasty's influence on classical music through the years should not be underestimated. Johann Sebastian had twenty children of whom Wilhelm Friedemann, Carl Philipp Emmanuel, Johann Christian and Johann Christoph were all composers. Johann Sebastian didn't show terribly much imagination in naming his kids – five of them were called Johann and one Johanna.

Check it out

Brandenburg Concertos | *Toccata and Fugue* in D minor (perfect music for Vincent Price in the film *The Phantom of the Opera*) | *Sheep May Safely Graze*

Well I never!

Bach was a fan of two things – coffee and numbers. Lots of his pieces play games with numbers, inaudibly. And he wrote a whole cantata about coffee.

★ ★ ★

Samuel BARBER (1910–81)

One of the most popular American composers, Samuel Barber is best known for his *Adagio for Strings*, which was used to great effect by the director Oliver Stone in his Vietnam War movie, *Platoon*. More recently, his hauntingly beautiful *Violin Concerto*, composed on the death of his mother, has become a firm Classic FM favourite.

Not to be confused with: *The Barber of Seville*, which is an opera by Rossini, nor with *Babar the Elephant*, which is a piece for voice and piano (or orchestra) by Poulenc.

 Namedrop Toscanini, the conductor, whose idea it was to re-orchestrate the slow movement of his String Quartet. This became 'the Barber *Adagio*', as it's now known.

★ ★ ★

John BARRY (born 1933)

British composer who made his name with his music for films. More recently he has had a number of big hits with his CDs of orchestral music. His style is very lush, almost epic, and he has a talent for very hummable tunes.

 Check it out *The Beyondness of Things | Dances with Wolves*

★ ★ ★

Ludwig van BEETHOVEN (1770–1827)

Along with Mozart, Beethoven has a strong claim on the title 'the world's greatest classical composer'. He wrote everything: concertos, operas, choral works, pieces for solo instruments – you name it – but his speciality was the symphony. He led a tough life, often beaten, early on, by his alcoholic father. In his twenties, his doctor told him that he was going deaf and by the time he was in his thirties, he had totally lost his hearing.

The supreme quality of the works which he wrote and never actually heard remains one of the great marvels of classical music. By the time his magnificent *Ninth Symphony* received its premiere, he was completely deaf. For the first public performance, he sat on the stage with his back to the audience. At the end of the concert, it was only when one of the singers turned him around to face the crowd that he realised that they had been wildly cheering and applauding his masterpiece.

His best known work for solo piano, the *'Moonlight' Sonata*, wasn't given the name by Beethoven himself. It acquired the title from a critic, who thought that the piece evoked an image of the moon over Lake Lucerne.

Beethoven's *Third Symphony* was going to be dedicated to Napoleon Bonaparte. But when the composer heard that his hero had crowned himself Emperor, he ran to his manuscript and crossed out the dedication. In its place he put *'Eroica'* (the hero), adding the words 'to the memory of a great man'.

Fellow composer Franz Schubert was one of the pall-bearers at Beethoven's funeral. In total, more than 30,000 people paid their respects to Ludwig at the service.

Check it out

Symphony No. 5, which must have the most famous opening bars in all classical music | *Symphony No. 6 ('Pastoral')* | *Symphony No. 9 ('Choral')* – particularly the magnificent final movement, the 'Ode to Joy'

★ ★ ★

Hector BERLIOZ (1803–69)

If you are looking for a 'patron saint of the romantic period', then you could do worse than light upon floppy-fringed Frenchman, Hector Berlioz. Hector was a bit of a luvvie, and, indeed, Hector's house was often home to some rather wild, over-dramatic behaviour. He once pursued an ex-lover with pistols and poison. Another he followed disguised as a maid. Say no more.

Check it out

Symphonie fantastique | the oratorio *The Childhood of Christ* | his *Requiem*, which was written for a HUGE chorus and orchestra as well as four brass bands – one at each corner of the stage

Namedrop

Harriet Smithson, the Irish actress Berlioz was nuts about. He wooed her, won her and wed her. Of course, then he got bored of her and started craving other women. An artist's life, eh?

★ ★ ★

Leonard BERNSTEIN (1918–90)

This American composer's biggest hit was the musical *West Side Story*. Bernstein wrote the music and Stephen Sondheim wrote the words – what a partnership! He also spent a lot of his life touring as a very successful conductor.

Check it out

His overture to *Candide* and see if you can stop your foot from tapping | *Chichester Psalms*, beautiful music written to a commission from the Dean of Chichester in the 1960s

★ ★ ★

Georges BIZET (1838–75)

Another romantic Frenchman. His best-known work is the opera *Carmen*. It tells the story of a beautiful woman who not only seduces a soldier then dumps him for a matador, but who also works in a cigarette factory. (See page 88). Despite the popularity of *Carmen*, it's another work of Bizet's which is the Classic FM listeners' favourite duet of all time, 'Au fond du temple saint', from his opera *The Pearl Fishers*. Although *Carmen* is a huge hit now, poor Bizet popped his chaussures while it was still a bit of a flop.

Check it out

L'Arlésienne Suite No. 1 | *Jeux d'enfants* – ten piano pieces, five of which Bizet wrote out for orchestra

★ ★ ★

Luigi BOCCHERINI (1743–1805)

Boccherini is best known for the *Minuet* from his String Quintet No. 5, which is just one of a total of 154 quintets he wrote for various different combinations of instruments. One out of 154. Life can be cruel, can't it?

Check it out

Cello Concerto in G (Boccherini himself was a bit of a whizz on the cello)

★ ★ ★

Alexander BORODIN (1833–87)

Borodin was only a part-time composer. His day job was as a highly respected scientist in Russia. As a result, his first published work was a scientific paper, rather than a piece of music. His opera Prince Igor was actually completed after he had died, by composers Nikolai Rimsky-Korsakov and Alexander Glazounoff.

Check it out

Polovtsian Dances from *Prince Igor* | *In the Steppes of Central Asia* | *On the Action of Ethyl-iodide on Hydrobenzamide and Amarien* (his first work)

Namedrop

The musical *Kismet*, which is based on Borodin's tunes.

Johannes BRAHMS (1833–97)

Now known to many as one half of the rhyming slang for 'drunk', in his early career Brahms earned a living playing piano in brothels around his native Hamburg. He continued to tour as a pianist and was regarded as master of every type of music, except for opera, to which he never turned his hand. Brahms may have been musical in the daytime, but at night his snoring was a far from sweet sound. One conductor, forced to share a room with him, described how 'the mostly unearthly noises issued from his nasal and vocal organs'.

Brahms would never have won the award for 'best-turned-out composer'. He seems to have had particular problems in the trouser department. He hated buying new clothes and often wore baggy trousers which were covered in patches and nearly always too short. Once, his trousers nearly fell down altogether in the middle of a performance. On another occasion, he took a tie from around his neck and looped it around his waist in place of a belt.

Brahms wrote his *Academic Festival Overture* to celebrate being given an honourary degree by the University of Bremen. At its first performance, the largely student audience were delighted to hear the tune to their favourite student song *Gaudeamus igitur* included in the music. It's said that they cheered and threw their hats in the air.

Check it out

Hungarian Dance No. 5 | Piano Concerto No. 1 | Symphony No. 4 | Violin Concerto

Namedrop

(1) Clara Schumann. Brahms was quite besotted with her, and probably wanted the relationship to go further after her husband Robert had died.

(2) Johann Strauss II. Despite the difference in their music, these two were firm friends. When Mrs Strauss once asked Brahms for an autograph, he wrote out a few bars of *The Blue Danube*, with the note 'Sadly, not by Brahms!'

Benjamin BRITTEN (1913–76)

This composer has possibly the most appropriate sounding surname ever, as he seems to stand for everything that was Britain in the mid-20th century. For much of his life he lived in Aldeburgh, on the Suffolk coast, where he founded the music festival that still continues every year, in June. He is buried in Aldeburgh church, beside his partner, the tenor Peter Pears.

Check it out

For a great introduction to Britten, try something like the *Sea Interludes* from *Peter Grimes* or the *Ceremony of Carols* | If you'd like to delve a little deeper, try the *Serenade for tenor, horn and strings*, written for Pears.

Well I never!

Britten was a conscientious objector during World War Two. He was excused military service in exchange for his participation in official state music making.

★ ★ ★

Max BRUCH (1838–1920)

This German composer is best known for his *Violin Concerto No. 1*. It's been voted the UK's favourite piece of classical music no fewer than five times in the annual Classic FM Hall of Fame poll. As well as composing, Bruch spent three years in Liverpool as the Music Director of the Royal Liverpool Philharmonic, now Classic FM's Orchestra in the North-West.

Check it out

Scottish Fantasy | *Kol Nidrei*

★ ★ ★

Anton BRUCKNER (1824–96)

Anton Bruckner was a simple man, racked with self-doubt. So much so that he abandoned working on his first symphony, thinking it not good enough. He started on his second, which he called his first symphony. When he later went back to complete his original symphony, he called it *Die Nulte* which translates as something like The Nothingth or The Zeroth.

Check it out
Symphony No. 7 in E | Symphony No. 8 in C minor

Well I never!
If you ever go to the monastery of St Florian in Vienna, have a look at the organ. Bruckner is buried under it.

★ ★ ★

Frédéric CHOPIN (1810–49)

Chopin was sort of the Henry Ford of composers, whose catchphrase might have been 'you can have any instrument as long as it's the piano'. Some would say he was a little obsessive about tinkling the ivories, writing no fewer than 169 different pieces for solo piano. And now for some trivia. His *Second Piano Concerto* was actually written before his *First Piano Concerto*. But his *First Piano Concerto* was published first, so even though the *Second Piano Concerto* was in fact written first, it has always been referred to as the second. This seemed to happen quite a lot with composers (see Bruckner, above).

Check it out
Nocturne No. 2 | *Prelude* No. 15 (*'The Raindrop'*) | *Waltz* No. 6 (*'The Minute Waltz'* – which, in fact, usually takes about a minute and a half to play)

Namedrop
George Sand, the pseudonym of the female novelist with whom Chopin had a long and stormy affair.

★ ★ ★

Aaron COPLAND (1900–90)

This American composer's best-known work, *Fanfare for the Common Man*, provides a stirring brassy opening to many public events in the USA. At their inauguration, presidents swear by it. Although Copland is thought of as being as American as apple pie, his parents were in fact both Russian and his original name was Kaplan.

Check it out

The ballet suites *Rodeo* and *Appalachian Spring*

Well I never!

In the 1950s, Copland was hauled in front of the 'witchhunt' committee of Joseph McCarthy, suspected of un-American activities. Copland gave as good as he got and was not asked to reappear.

★ ★ ★

Sir Peter Maxwell DAVIES (born 1934)

The current Master of the Queen's Music has had a long career composing critically acclaimed works. He is the founder of the St Magnus Festival in Orkney, the Scottish islands where he has lived since 1971.

Check it out

Farewell to Stromness, a solo piano piece performed by the composer, has captured the imagination of Classic FM listeners. It was written as a protest against a nuclear reprocessing plant on one of the Orkney isles. | *The Manchester Group*, the name of the group of composers and musicians in which he first came to prominence, including fellow modernist Sir Harrison Birtwistle.

Namedrop

Everyone refers to Sir Peter simply as 'Max'.

★ ★ ★

Claude DEBUSSY (1862–1918)

Debussy saw himself as a very French musician. He was friendly with many of the impressionist painters, which resulted in his work being given an 'impressionist' tag. In fact, he wasn't really doing an impression of anyone – he was an innovator whose musical style paved the way for other 20th-century composers. His lover, Gaby, shot herself when he ended their relationship to set up home with his first wife, Rosalie. Gaby survived her suicide attempt. Five years later, he left Rosalie for the woman who would become his second wife. Just like Gaby, Rosalie shot herself and she, too, lived to tell the tale. The moral of the story? Never marry someone who's a good shot.

Check it out
Clair de lune | La Mer | Prélude à l'après-midi d'un faune

Well I never!
Debussy was staying at the Grand Hotel, Eastbourne, in 1905, when he put the finishing touches to *La Mer*.

★ ★ ★

Léo DELIBES (1836–91)

Delibes's opera *Lakmé* soared to new heights of popularity on the back of the long-running British Airways advertising campaign, which features the opera's most famous tune, the *Flower Duet*. His other popular composition is the ballet *Coppélia*, which tells the story of a toymaker and his dancing doll.

Check it out
Yet another ballet, *Sylvia*

Namedrop
Berlioz and Bizet, both of whom were Delibes's bosses when he was chorus master at Paris's Théâtre Lyrique

★ ★ ★

Frederick DELIUS (1862–1934)

Born in Bradford, Delius decided to become a composer in his twenties when he was running an orange plantation in Florida. In his latter years he suffered severely from the syphilis which he had picked up when in Paris in the 1890s. He was forced to dictate his music to his scribe, Eric Fenby, without whom we'd have neither lots of the late Delius output, nor any knowledge of the word 'amanuensis'.

Delius's intermezzo *The Walk to the Paradise Garden* sounds particularly idyllic, especially coming as it does from the opera *A Village Romeo and Juliet*. Sounds idyllic, that is, until you realise that the Paradise Garden is a pub. They're off for a pint!

Check it out

La Calinda | *On Hearing the First Cuckoo in Spring* | *The Walk to the Paradise Garden* | If you are feeling adventurous, try a live performance of *A Mass of Life*, Delius's choral masterpiece. It's the musical equivalent of going over a waterfall in a barrel. Marvellous.

Namedrop

Ken Russell, who made a film of Delius's life called *A Song of Summer*.

★ ★ ★

Antonín DVOŘÁK (1841–1904)

Dvořák loved his Czech homeland and was terribly homesick when he moved to the USA for three years in the 1890s. While he was there though, he discovered American folk melodies. These tunes heavily influenced him while he was writing his best-known work, the *New World Symphony* (Symphony No. 9). For many people in the UK , the slow movement of this symphony will forever be associated with wholemeal bread and North Yorkshire streets, after it was used in adverts for Hovis.

Away from music, Dvořák was a committed trainspotter. He would practise his hobby at the Franz Josef Station in Prague; it's said he knew the train timetable off by heart. But he was, after all, only living up to his name (remove the middle 'tonínDv' …).

When Dvořák was once staying in London – to oversee a performance of his piano concerto at Crystal Palace – he was thrown out of the Athenaeum Club. He'd mistaken it for a coffee house and was immediately evicted.

Check it out

Song to the Moon from the opera *Rusalka* | *Serenade for Strings* | *Slavonic Dances*

Well I never!

Dvořák (and Mrs Dvořák, for that matter) liked to get up very early indeed. When they stayed with composer and organist Charles Villiers Stanford in Cambridge, he was more than a little surprised that, when he woke at 6 am, the Dvořáks were already to be found sitting under a tree in his garden.

★ ★ ★

Ludovico EINAUDI (born 1955)

This Italian pianist and composer is now a firm favourite with Classic FM listeners. He has become known particularly for his beautifully haunting melodies for solo piano.

Check it out

Stanze | *Le onde* | *Eden Roc* | *I giorni* | *Una mattina*

Sir Edward ELGAR (1857–1934)

One of the greatest British composers, Elgar is quite rightly regarded as a national treasure. He spent much of his life living in his native Worcestershire and the beautiful surrounding English countryside inspired him to write many of the most quintessentially English tunes. And his handlebar moustache is to die for. See for yourself by taking a look at the back of a twenty-pound note. The reason the Royal Mint chose him? The detail on his big bushy moustache would be difficult for conterfeiters to forge.

When Elgar wrote his *Variations on an Original Theme*, it was dubbed the *Enigma Variations* because every movement depicted one of his friends, each of whom was labelled only with initials. The bigger enigma is the identity of the 'original' theme. Some think it's based on a famous tune, some think that it's a well-known melody reversed and altered, others say that the 'enigma' tune is not played but just fits alongside the tune Elgar wrote. Who knows?

Check it out

Cello Concerto | *Chanson de matin* | *Pomp and Circumstance March* No. 1 (the tune to 'Land of Hope and Glory') | *Salut d'amour* | *Serenade for Strings*

Well I never!

When the composer Dvořák came over to England to conduct his Sixth Symphony in Worcester Shire Hall, one of the rank of first violins was none other than Edward Elgar. Elgar loved the work: '… simply ravishing', he wrote.

★ ★ ★

Gabriel FAURÉ (1845–1924)

Best known for his *Requiem*, which is undoubtedly one of the great choral masterpieces, Fauré is far better known in his homeland, where he is more or less the French Elgar. Both composers had their religious faith tested in later life. Faure's instrumental music is definitely worth a listen.

Check it out
Pavane | Cantique de Jean Racine | Dolly Suite

Well I never!
Just like Beethoven, Fauré battled against increasing deafness, and wrote his last few works without being able to hear a thing.

★ ★ ★

César FRANCK (1822–90)

Here is one of those rarest of beasts – a famous Belgian. And unlike Hercule Poirot or Tintin, César Franck actually existed. He never really had much success with his music during his life. In fact, the first glimmer of critical approval only came in the weeks before he died.

Check it out
Panis angelicus – a wedding classic | Symphonic Variations for Piano and Orchestra

★ ★ ★

George GERSHWIN (1898–1937)

Despite being written in the early part of the 20th century, Gershwin's music sounds very fresh and contemporary today. He was the master of fusing together jazz and classical music and was earning as much as $250,000 a year at the height of his popularity, which must make him one of the most financially successful of any composer in their own lifetime.

Check it out

Rhapsody in Blue | Piano Concerto in F | his opera *Porgy and Bess* which includes the hit songs 'Summertime' and 'I got plenty o' nuttin'' | *An American in Paris* – great musical pictures painted for orchestra.

Well I never!

Gershwin wrote a song called 'I'm a poached egg!' It's a love song, apparently, in which the singer compares his feelings of being without his loved one as being similar to a poached egg, separated from its toast.

★ ★ ★

Philip GLASS (born 1937)

Arguably one of the most respected living American composers, Glass's music receives its widest audience through his film soundtracks. He belongs to the group of composers known as 'minimalists', whose music is made up of simple rhythms, repeated over and over again.

Check it out

Violin Concerto | *Koyaanisqatsi* | *The Hours* | *Kundun*

★ ★ ★

Alexander GLAZOUNOFF (1865–1936)

Glazounoff's influence on Russian music was greater than just the sum total of his own work. He studied with Rimsky-Korsakov when he was just a teenager and counted Prokofieff, Stravinsky and Shostakovich among his own pupils later in life.

Check it out

> *The Seasons* | If you're feeling braver, his one-movement Alto Saxophone Concerto is fab.

★ ★ ★

Henryk GÓRECKI (born 1933)

This Polish composer shot to fame back in 1992 when Classic FM started to play a recording of his Symphony No. 3 featuring the soprano Dawn Upshaw with the London Sinfonietta. The second movement of this 'Symphony of Sorrowful Songs' is a particular favourite. None of his other music has come anywhere close to repeating this success. And don't let the name catch you out – even though it doesn't look like it, it's pronounced 'Goretski'.

Check it out

> *Totus Tuus*, a haunting and striking hymn to the Virgin Mary, written for an open-air mass celebrated by the late Pope John Paul II.

Well I never!

> The heart-rending second movement of the *Symphony of Sorrowful Songs* is a setting of a prayer found scratched into a cell wall of the Nazi Gestapo's headquarters, written by a young girl in the Second World War.

★ ★ ★

Charles GOUNOD (1818–93)

Gounod was writing music in Paris at the time when it was a seething hotbed of great romantic composers. His contemporaries include Chopin, Liszt and Berlioz. His most famous work is the opera *Faust*, which spawned the Jewel Song and The Soldiers' Chorus. But Classic FM listeners' favourite Gounod piece has proved to be 'Judex' from his little-known oratorio, *Mors et Vita*.

Check it out

Ave Maria (Gounod borrowed Bach's Prelude No. 1 and put a second tune over the top of it)

Namedrop

Alfred Hitchcock. Gounod's *Funeral March of a Marionette* was used as the theme to the TV series 'Alfred Hitchcock presents …'

★ ★ ★

Edvard GRIEG (1843–1907)

Grieg is Norway's most famous musical son, although the Scots could lay some claim to him being one of their own because his Scottish great-grandfather emigrated to Scandinavia after the Battle of Culloden. Many of his tunes contain soaring melodies that evoke his Norwegian home.

Check it out

Piano Concerto | *Holberg Suite* | *Peer Gynt Suites* Nos. 1 and 2 (the first includes the hits *Morning* and *In the Hall of the Mountain King*)

Well I never!

Grieg was given an honourary degree by Cambridge University in 1894. Straight after the ceremony, he rushed to the post office and sent a telegram to a friend, a medical doctor in Bergen who shared his surname. He signed his telegram 'Doctor Grieg'.

★ ★ ★

George Frideric HANDEL (1685–1759)

Handel showed great talent as a youngster, but he had to suffer for his art. He was forced to sneak a small keyboard up to the loft of his house to practise on, because his father wouldn't let him go near a musical instrument.

In a way, he was the Greg Rusedski of classical music. Although he was German, he was considered one of Britain's great composers, after becoming a British citizen. This came to pass when the Elector of Hanover was promoted to the job of being King George I. His music includes opera and instrumental work, but he's probably best known for his great big choral masterpieces, which are still regularly performed up and down the country today.

His *Music for the Royal Fireworks* was written for a display put on by King George II in London's Hyde Park. The music might have proved to be a hit, but the fireworks definitely weren't. That's all except one particular Catherine wheel, which was what you might call a 'direct hit'. It set fire to a wooden tower and caused pandemonium among the crowds.

While he was in Italy, Handel was challenged to a duel – with a difference. The composer Domenico Scarlatti dared him to agree to a 'keyboard duel' – Handel on organ, Scarlatti on harpsichord. The result was a fudge: Handel was declared the better organist, Scarlatti the better harpsichordist.

Check it out

Messiah | 'Ombra mai fu' from the opera *Xerxes* | *Zadok the Priest* (used in the film *The Madness of King George*) | *Water Music* | *Arrival of the Queen of Sheba* from the oratorio *Solomon*

Well I never!

Handel was reputedly a big chap with an enormous appetite. In one restaurant, he booked a table for four and ordered four meals. When the waiter arrived with four feasts and enquired after his other guests, Handel barked at him to put the food down and rapidly gobbled the lot.

★ ★ ★

Joseph HAYDN (1732–1809)

Now to say that Haydn was hard-working would be a dramatic understatement. During the 77 years of his life he wrote no fewer than 104 symphonies, more than 80 string quartets, over 50 piano sonatas, at least 24 concertos and 20 operas. And we haven't even got started on the choral and chamber pieces yet.

When he was a youngster Haydn was a chorister at St Stephen's Cathedral in Vienna. He had a fantastic singing voice. So, when his choirmaster suggested that if he had a small operation he would be able to keep his unbroken voice for the rest of his life, the young Joseph liked the sound of the idea. It was only when his horrified father discovered that his son was about to go under the surgeon's knife that the boy was told what the operation would actually entail.

Later in life, Haydn befriended many famous people and when Lord Nelson and Lady Hamilton visited him in 1800, they got on like a house on fire, exchanging gossip and gifts. Haydn had his new mass performed during the visit and the new work gained the nickname of the 'Nelson Mass'.

Very often neglected in favour of his counterparts, Mozart and Beethoven, it is often said that Haydn is a composer you learn to appreciate more with age.

Haydn's Cello Concerto No. 1 in C spent 177 years in obscurity. Once composed, it was lost until 1961, when it was found in the Prague National Museum.

Check it out

The magnificent choral work *The Creation* | Symphony No. 94 in G, known as the *'Surprise Symphony'* because of the deafening chord that comes crashing in after a very quiet opening | Cello Concertos Nos. 1 & 2 | *The Seasons*

Namedrop

The German National Anthem. Haydn wrote the music, originally as a part of his String Quartet in C, and various words were added at later stages.

★ ★ ★

Gustav HOLST (1874–1934)

One of those One-Hit-Wonders, Gustav Holst is famous for writing *The Planets*. Six of the seven movements represent the astrological influences of the planets: Mars (war), Venus (peace), Jupiter (jollity), Uranus (magic), Saturn (old age) and Neptune (mysticism). The other movement is reserved for Mercury, the winged messenger of the gods. Pluto fails to make the line up, mainly because it had not yet been discovered. The great hymn and rugby anthem 'I vow to thee my country' is sung to the tune of Jupiter.

Check it out

The *St Paul's Suite*, which Holst wrote for his pupils at St Paul's Girls School in London, where he was Director of Music for nearly thirty years.

Well I never!

Despite being viewed now as almost quintessentially English, Holst felt forced to change from Gustavus von Holst to simply Gustav Holst, to offset the German-sounding nature of his name, during the First World War.

★ ★ ★

James HORNER (born 1953)

One of the most commercially successful film composers, James Horner has scored more than a hundred films. He has won three Grammy Awards, two Academy Awards and has a further five Oscar nominations and four Golden Globe nominations. He is far and away best known for his score to *Titanic*.

Check it out

Apollo 13 | Braveheart | Field of Dreams | A Beautiful Mind | The Perfect Storm | The Missing | The Mask of Zorro | Iris

Namedrop

Spectral Shimmers, one of the few pieces of non-film music Horner has written. It was premiered by the Indianapolis Symphony Orchestra.

★ ★ ★

Karl JENKINS (born 1944)

Karl Jenkins has had a varied career, ranging from being principal oboist in the National Youth Orchestra to being a leading member of the seventies' rock outfit Soft Machine. *Adiemus: Songs of Sanctuary* was an instant hit with Classic FM listeners back in 1995 and, like much of Jenkins' music, has become even more famous through being used in TV advertising campaigns. More recently, the Sanctus from *The Armed Man: A Mass for Peace* has achieved a kind of cult status with listeners.

Check it out

Palladio | Requiem

Well I never!

Karl's recording studio in central London is called Moustache Studios, a reference to his Elgar-like, handlebar lip cover.

★ ★ ★

Leoš JANÁČEK (1854–1928)

If you ever happen to be seated next to the Moravian Ambassador at a sit-down dinner, then you could do worse than namedrop Janáček. Alongside his Czech mates, Dvořák and Smetana, he flew the flag for his homeland, musically speaking. He was in his fifties before he achieved any real recognition.

Check it out

The *Sinfonietta*, which stumped up the opening theme tune for the ultimate school skive television series of the 1970s, *Crown Court* | *Jenůfa*, his most famous opera

★ ★ ★

Aram KHACHATURIAN (1903–78)

Two pieces of music written for separate ballets top the list of this Armenian composer's most played work. The *Sabre Dance* from *Gayaneh* may have made him famous around the globe just after it was written in the 1940s – now used for an Adidas advert – but for a whole generation he will always be the man behind the theme tune to *The Onedin Line*. This piece's real name is the *Adagio of Spartacus and Phrygia*.

Check it out

Galop from *Masquerade*

Well I never!

Khachaturian's first instrument was a tuba

★ ★ ★

Ruggero LEONCAVALLO (1857–1919)

Leoncavallo had a stroke of bad luck when he was writing an opera, which he hoped would launch him on the road to fame and fortune. The trouble was that Puccini got there first with his version of *La Bohème*, and the critics and audiences judged it to be better than Leoncavallo's composition. He did have one notable success, an opera called *Pagliacci*, which includes the tenor aria 'Vesti la giubba', which continues to be among the most popular of any in the operatic repertoire.

Well I never!

Queen's 1984 hit *It's a Hard Life* starts with a snippet of *Vesti la giubba*, sung to the words 'I don't want my freedom, there's no reason for living …'

★ ★ ★

Franz LISZT (1811–86)

One of the great pianists of his time, a performance by Liszt was greeted by the sort of response that we would associate with a chart-topping pop superstar today. He enjoyed the rock 'n' roll lifestyle a good century before it had been invented and had a long list of sexual conquests – even after he took holy orders. He had a penchant for huge, flashy versions of other people's pieces. Like olives, they are an acquired taste.

Check it out

Hungarian Rhapsody No. 2 | *Liebestraum No. 3* | *Piano Sonata* | *Rhapsodie espagnole*

Well I never!

When you go to see a piano concerto in concert, the position of the piano in relation to the orchestra is all down to Liszt. Up until he performed, the pianist used to face the audience. As the first real megastar of the piano, the heartthrob pianist decided he wanted to be seen by his fans so had the piano moved side on – and it stuck.

★ ★ ★

Gustav MAHLER (1860–1911)

A renowned conductor during his lifetime, particularly of opera, Mahler only rose to real popularity as a composer during the latter half of the 20th century. He was a tortured soul who was analysed by Freud. His biggest hit is the *Adagietto* from his Symphony No. 5. He wrote nine symphonies, which seems to be the number to write – Beethoven and Dvořák also wrote nine.

Check it out
> Symphony No. 1 (known as 'The Titan') | Symphony No. 2 ('The Resurrection') | Symphony No. 8 (known as 'The Symphony of a Thousand' because of the vast number of musicians needed to perform it)

Namedrop
> Robert Powell, who played Mahler in the 1974 Ken Russell movie.

★ ★ ★

Pietro MASCAGNI (1863–1945)

This Italian One-Hit-Wonder is best known for his opera *Cavalleria Rusticana*. But rather than a famous aria, it's the Intermezzo (the bit in the middle) that is most often heard today. When this opera is performed in full, it tends to be paired up with another One-Hit-Wonder, Leoncavallo's *Pagliacci* – a double-act known as 'Cav & Pag'.

It's actually down to Mrs Mascagni that Pietro became well known at all. His wife secretly entered *Cavalleria Rusticana* for a competition after the composer himself decided that it wasn't anywhere near good enough to win. It ended up taking top honours and Mr and Mrs Mascagni's lives were transformed by the prize money. The poor old chap never managed to write another hit to rival it though.

Check it out
> Er, that's it.

★ ★ ★

Jules MASSENET (1842–1912)

Much like Mascagni, Massenet is most famous for a piece of incidental music from an opera – this time, it's the gentle *Meditation* from *Thaïs*. Sadly, as far as we know, he never wrote a 'mass in A', thus depriving the world of Massenet's *Mass in A*. Which, were it to receive an afternoon performance, would be Massenet's *Mass in A* matinee.

Check it out

Manon, fantastic opera using the same story as Puccini's *Manon Lescaut*, but nearly a decade earlier.

★ ★ ★

Sir Paul McCARTNEY (born 1942)

Although Sir Paul McCartney's best-known compositions were co-written with John Lennon in the sixties, a few years ago he carved out a new career for himself by turning his hand to classical music. His classical works have proved that his knack for writing a strong, catchy melody has not deserted him.

In fact, the Fab Four's links to classical music go back a long way – Beethoven's Ninth Symphony and part of Wagner's *Lohengrin* both feature in the Beatles' movie *Help*.

Check it out

Liverpool Oratorio | *The Leaf* | *Standing Stone* | *Working Classical* | *A Garland for Linda*, a collection of ten pieces for his late wife by various composers, for which McCartney himself wrote *Nova*.

Namedrop

John Rutter, who also contributed a piece to *A Garland for Linda*, and is a big Beatles fan.

★ ★ ★

Felix MENDELSSOHN (1809–47)

This German-born composer was a frighteningly clever child, excelling as a painter, poet, athlete, linguist and musician. He made his public debut as a pianist at the age of nine and by the time he was sixteen he had composed his *Octet for Strings*.

When he was 17, Mendelssohn composed the overture to Shakespeare's play *A Midsummer Night's Dream*. It took him another 17 years to get around to composing the rest of the incidental music to the play. Many brides and bridegrooms will be thankful that he did – the music he wrote includes the ubiquitous *Wedding March*, heard at marriage services up and down the country every week.

A tour of Scotland in 1829 resulted in the hugely popular *Hebrides Overture*. His music tends to be bright and cheerful – indeed his name, Felix, means happy in Latin – but he died at a tragically young age, only 38, having never really recovered from the death of his much-loved sister, Fanny, who was also a gifted musician.

Check it out

O for the wings of a dove | *Songs without Words* | Symphony No. 4 ('Italian') | Violin Concerto

Well I never!

Just like Beethoven's *Moonlight Sonata*, all but a handful of Mendelssohn's Songs without Words have a title made up by a publisher. So, *Restlessness*, *The Fleecy Clouds*, *The Shepherd's Complaint* (for which he no doubt had an ointment) are all the work of a publisher's imagination.

★ ★ ★

Modest MOUSSORGSKY (1839–81)

Moussorgsky was a high-ranking official in the Russian guards and his story is one of riches to rags. As a young adult, he was quite a man about town, but, by the time he died at the age of 42, he had descended into alcohol-induced poverty. Hence, in the most common picture of him, he has a bright red nose.

Not all Moussorgsky's works were 100% Moussorgsky. His friend Rimsky-Korsakov helped him out by orchestrating lots of his opera *Boris Godounov*, as he did with his *Night on a Bare Mountain*. And his *Pictures at an Exhibition* is best known in its version orchestrated by Ravel.

Check it out

Take a look at Walt Disney's cartoon masterpiece *Fantasia* to see and hear *Night on a Bare Mountain* at its best

Namedrop

'The Mighty Handful', also known as 'The Mighty Five' – the name given to the group of five composers to which he belonged. Balakirev, Borodin, Cui and Rimsky-Korsakov were the others

★ ★ ★

Wolfgang Amadeus MOZART (1756–91)

You might know him as Wolfgang Amadeus Mozart – but his real name in full is Johannes Chrysostomus Wolfgangus Theophilus Mozart. 'Amadeus' is the Latin version of the Greek word 'Theophilus', which means 'love of God'.

When those in the know sit down to debate 'Who's the greatest of them all?' Mozart and Beethoven usually end up coming first and second, although the top spot changes hands as often as a magician's playing card. Probably the best-known child prodigy, Mozart could play the keyboard by the age of three and could compose from five. He went on his first European tour when he was six and by the time he had reached the grand old age of twelve, he had finished two operas.

Mozart's dad, Leopold, loved to show off his son's talents as a way of making money. When the prodigy was just seven years old, his party trick was to cover the piano keyboard with a cloth and then to play fiendishly difficult pieces without being able to see any of the notes.

Mozart wrote five horn concertos during his relatively short life, so it's hard to believe that when he was a small boy he was absolutely terrified of the instrument. One musician described how, when he blew his horn in Wolfgang's direction, the colour instantly drained out of the boy's cheeks. The horn player seriously thought the young Mozart would have suffered a fit had he not stopped playing.

As an adult, Mozart could knock out a new piece of music in a matter of minutes. Once, when he was walking along the street, a beggar asked him for some money. Mozart was, as usual, a bit short of readies at the time, so he wrote out a tune on a piece of manuscript paper. He told the beggar to take it to a music publisher, who would exchange it for cash.

In the winter of 1781–82, Mozart was challenged to a keyboard duel by the composer and piano-maker, Clementi. It was officially a tie, but while Clementi was graciously wowed by Mozart's abilities, Mozart's views on the event verge on the catty. He said that Clementi was 'mechanical' and played with 'no feeling'.

Mozart became a Freemason in December 1784. His lodge was called Benificence, but later merged with two other lodges to form Newly-Crowned Hope. Mozart was an active member, writing a lot of music for Masonic events, as well as the opera *The Magic Flute*, a Masonic allegory.

Mozart's music is an excellent choice if you're planning to go to a live classical concert for the first time. It's nice to know that he did have some faults though – he was said to be very arrogant, had a strange obsession with his rear end and was hopeless at managing his money. He was buried in an unmarked pauper's grave.

Check it out

Laudate Dominum | *Requiem* | Clarinet Concerto in A | Piano Concerto No. 21 | Horn Concerto No. 4 | Piano Concerto No. 24 | Serenade No. 13 ('*Eine kleine Nachtmusik*') | Symphony No. 41 ('Jupiter') | *Cosi fan tutte* | *Don Giovanni* | *The Magic Flute* | *The Marriage of Figaro* | the film *Amadeus*

★ ★ ★

Michael NYMAN (born 1941)

This minimalist British composer has written many film soundtracks, the best known of which is *The Piano*. He later turned the score into a single movement Piano Concerto.

In Jane Campion's 1992 film, Holly Hunter was cast as a piano teacher. Hunter, a pianist herself, learnt to play Nyman's solo piano music in order that she might actually play the piano on set. So, to sum up, Holly Hunter, who plays the piano, plays the piano in *The Piano*. Glad we cleared that one up.

★ ★ ★

Jacques OFFENBACH (1819–80)

This is the man who let loose the *Can-Can* on an unsuspecting public back in 1858. It comes from the operetta *Orpheus in the Underworld*, which scandalised the chattering classes of Paris at the time of its premiere. Offenbach is also known for the *Barcarolle* from his opera *The Tales of Hoffman*. There used to be a strange association of bad luck attached to his name, a bit like Macbeth in the theatre, whereby people would have to cross themselves if he was mentioned. Staying with the name theme, Offenbach was born in the town of Cologne and sometimes he would sign himself as 'O. de Cologne'.

Well I never!

Offenbach was shunned by the Paris Opéra-Comique, who refused to perform his works. So he set up his own theatre, the Bouffes-Parisiens and, instantly, his music took off. Within months, he had to move to bigger premises to accommodate the huge audiences.

★ ★ ★

Carl ORFF (1895–1982)

Carl Orff's *Carmina Burana* sniffed out the sweet smell of popularity after advertising executives decided that the opening 'O fortuna' would be the perfect accompaniment to the crashing waves of an advertising campaign for Old Spice aftershave. And although it might sound all medieval and gothic (indeed, the words are quite saucy, in praise of wine, women and song), Orff died so recently that he may in fact have seen the Old Spice ad on the telly. Who knows? He himself may have splashed some on.

When *Carmina Burana* was first performed in 1937, it quickly became a hit. And Orff's reaction? He ordered his publisher to pulp every other work he had written up to that point.

 Well I never! Orff was an expert in the music of Monteverdi, and edited an edition of his works.

★ ★ ★

Johann PACHELBEL (1653–1706)

Another One-Hit-Wonder, this organist and composer is famous for his *Canon*. Just like Albinoni's *Adagio*, it only became mega-well-known more than a couple of hundred years after it was written. But, unlike Albinoni, it was at least all his own work. J S Bach was a big fan.

★ ★ ★

Niccolò PAGANINI (1782–1840)

As well as composing, Paganini was one of classical music's greatest showmen and is said to have been the fastest violinist ever. Officials once measured him doing twelve notes to the second. He, himself, encouraged the rumour that he had sold himself to the devil in exchange for his phenomenal fiddling fingers. One concert reviewer said he could see a small devil-like creature, perched on Paganini's shoulder, throughout a performance.

Check it out
Violin Concerto No. 1 in D | Violin Concerto No. 2 in B minor

Namedrop
Berlioz. Paganini commissioned the viola concerto *Harold in Italy* from Berlioz, but didn't like it when it arrived, so refused to pay or play. He later changed his mind, kneeling at Berlioz's feet and giving him a cheque for 20,000 francs.

★ ★ ★

Giovanni da PALESTRINA (1525-94)

The composer Palestrina wasn't called Palestrina. Sorry to shock you, but it's true. His name was Giovanni Pierluigi. He became known as Giovanni da Palestrina – John from Palestrina – because that was the small Italian town which he called home.

Palestrina's *Missa Papae Marcelli* – literally the Mass for Pope Marcellus – was never actually heard by its dedicatee. Pope Marcellus reigned for a mere 55 days before he died, never having got around to hearing the piece that carries his name.

Check it out
The *Missa Brevis* – a small and perfectly formed place to start

★ ★ ★

Arvo PÄRT (born 1935)

This Estonian composer sits alongside John Tavener, Henryk Górecki and John Rutter as one of the most popular modern choral writers. His laid-back, gentle sound is the musical equivalent of an empty, white room and appeals to 'chillout' enthusiasts just as much as to classical fans. To pronounce his name correctly, imagine a 'pear' then add a soft 't'. Pärt gives the impression of being a composer who is striving to write the perfect piece. Some would say he already has.

Check it out

Spiegel im Spiegel | if you're feeling more adventurous, try the *Cantus in Memoriam Benjamin Britten*, or *Tabula Rasa*.

★ ★ ★

Zbigniew PREISNER (born 1955)

When the *Requiem for my Friend* was released in 1996, it became an instant hit with Classic FM listeners. The friend in the title is the Polish film director Krzystof Kieslowski, he of the *Three Colours* trilogy fame, for whose movies Preisner had written the music.

Check it out

La double vie de Véronique (soundtrack) – cult movie with inherited cult status for its music.

★ ★ ★

Serge PROKOFIEFF (1891–1953)

This Russian composer suffered at the hands of Stalin, facing charges of composing music that worked against the State. Despite this, not only did he stay on in his homeland, but he also left us with many great tunes. Some were influenced by the time he spent in America and Europe during the early part of his adult life.

Prokofieff's *Troika* (sleigh ride) comes in the middle of his *Lieutenant Kijé Suite*. When most people listen to it, they think 'Christmas'. Russians, however, would be forgiven for thinking 'drink'. It's a reworking of an old Russian drinking song.

When Prokofieff wrote his music to *Romeo and Juliet* in 1935, some critics thought he had gone too far in terms of poetic licence. He'd changed one of the most famous endings in all literature – and had made it happy! In the face of almost universal disapproval, he changed it back again to Shakespeare's classic finish.

 Peter and the Wolf | the *Classical Symphony*, a sort of Prokofieff meets Mozart | *The Love for Three Oranges*, an opera, which has some great orchestral sections.

★ ★ ★

Giacomo PUCCINI (1858–1924)

Puccini took the opera baton from Verdi and ran with it, writing hit aria after hit aria. *La Bohème*, *Tosca* and *Madam Butterfly* are quite possibly the three most performed operas today. He also penned the aria that, for many people, simply is opera – 'Nessun Dorma' from *Turandot*. This song, made famous by the Three Tenors at the 1990 World Cup Finals in Italy, brought classical music into millions of people's lives.

Whenever Puccini came to London, he always liked to stay at the Savoy, savouring the luxury. On one occasion, in the summer of 1911, he availed himself of the in-house barbers, only to find himself sat in a chair next to Guglielmo Marconi, a fellow Italian and the inventor of the radio.

Right at the end of *Tosca*, the eponymous heroine meets a rather sudden end by jumping from the parapet of a prison, moments after her lover Mario has met his death at the hands of a firing squad. Usually there's a mattress back stage to lessen the impact of the singer's fall. On more than one occasion, the tragedy has turned to hilarity as the heroine hurls herself off the parapet, only to bounce back into the audience's view.

Puccini himself died before he could finish writing his opera *Turandot*. Another composer wrote the ending. At the premiere, the conductor Arturo Toscanini stopped the orchestra playing exactly at the point where Puccini stopped composing, turned to the audience and said: 'Here, death triumphed over art.'

Check it out

'Che gelida manina' and 'O soave fanciulla' from *La Bohème* | 'O mio babbino caro' from *Gianni Schicchi* | 'Un bel di' and *The Humming Chorus* from *Madam Butterfly* | 'Vissi d'arte' from *Tosca*

Namedrop

Franco Alfano, the man who finished off *Turandot* when the composer died leaving it unfinished

Well I never!

When Al Jolson wrote his hit song *Avalon* in 1920, Puccini was not one of those who found his foot tapping. His publishers, Ricordi, sued Jolson, saying it sounded like Puccini's aria *E lucevan le stelle*, from *Tosca*. They won, too, and were awarded $25,000 damages and all future royalties to the song.

★ ★ ★

Henry PURCELL (1659–95)

Often referred to as the first Great English Composer, Purcell was an amazing young talent, becoming Organist of Westminster Abbey – a top job – by the time he was 20. Despite the fact that he only lived for another 16 years, he had a busy old time of it, composing every conceivable type of music.

Check it out

'When I am laid in earth' (known as 'Dido's Lament') from *Dido and Aeneas* | the *Rondo* from *Abdelazar* | *Trumpet Tune and Air in D* | *Come Ye Sons of Art*

Well I never!

The huge void left after the death of Purcell, not filled until the arrival of Elgar some 200 years later (if you don't count the naturalised Handel) led England to be dubbed 'the land without music'

★ ★ ★

Serge RACHMANINOFF (1873–1943)

Rachmaninoff was one of those annoying people who wasn't just brilliant at one thing – he was top of the pile in three different areas. Today, we remember him as a composer, but in his day he was a fine conductor and magnificent concert pianist. He became best known as a performer when he moved to America. He made enough money to build a house in Los Angeles that was an exact replica of his original home back in Moscow.

Rachmaninoff's Piano Concerto No. 2 has regularly been voted number one in the Classic FM Hall of Fame and his Piano Concerto No. 3 shot to stardom after being included in the film *Shine*. He's also known for having one of the largest pairs of hands in classical music, which is why some of his piano pieces are fiendishly difficult for less well-endowed performers. He could cover twelve piano keys from the tip of his little finger to the tip of his thumb. That's around four keys more than average.

Rachmaninoff was once giving a recital in New York with fellow composer Fritz Kreisler. The former was on the piano and the latter on the violin. Kreisler got into a muddle about where he'd got to in the music. Panic-stricken, he whispered to Rachmaninoff, 'Where are we?' The whispered reply came back from Rachmaninoff: 'Carnegie Hall'.

Despite his success, Rachmaninoff seldom smiled in the photographs he left behind. Perhaps the Russians have no word for 'cheese'. Tall and severe, he was once dubbed 'a six-foot scowl'.

Check it out

Rhapsody on a Theme of Paganini | Symphony No. 2 | *Vocalise*

Namedrop

Lorelei, the name Rachmaninoff gave to his car. The composer was mad about cars (and later speedboats) and he was the first in his neighbourhood to have an automobile.

★ ★ ★

Maurice RAVEL (1875–1937)

A whole generation of people came across Ravel's music for the first time when Torvill and Dean skated their way to a gold medal accompanied by the *Bolero*. During the First World War, Ravel enlisted as an ambulance driver. He was deeply affected by the death and destruction that he witnessed, and the poignant *Le tombeau de Couperin* was his tribute not only to the French composer Couperin, but also to his fallen comrades.

Check it out

Pavane pour une infante défunte | the ballet *Daphnis and Chloé* | Piano Concerto for left hand which was written for a friend who lost an arm in the First World War.

Namedrop

Belvédère, Ravel's home near Paris, which was his pride and joy.

★ ★ ★

Nikolai RIMSKY-KORSAKOV (1844–1908)

A Russian naval officer turned music professor, Rimsky-Korsakov is best known for *Scheherezade*, which is based on the story of *The Arabian Nights*. When it came to knowing how to write brilliantly for orchestra, Rimsky-Korsakov was in a league of his own and also made quite a name for himself by arranging the work of other composers.

Check it out
Flight of the Bumble Bee | *Capriccio espagnol* | *Chant hindou* from his opera *Sadko*

Well I never!
Being a navy man, RK wrote some of his music while at sea. His Symphony in E flat was written while stationed off Gravesend in the Thames Estuary.

★ ★ ★

Joaquín RODRIGO (1901–99)

The *Concierto de Aranjuez* is this Spanish composer's greatest hit outside his home country. It's also the most popular piece for guitar and orchestra, having been 'covered' by so many people, from Miles Davis to the Grimethorpe Colliery Brass Band (as *Concerto de Orange Juice* in the film *Brassed Off*!)

Check it out
Fantasia para un Gentilhombre

Namedrop
Paul Dukas, writer of *The Sorcerer's Apprentice*, who was Rodrigo's teacher

★ ★ ★

Gioachino ROSSINI (1792–1868)

Another of the great Italian opera composers, Rossini was a one-man hit factory until he was 37. Then, suddenly, he stopped writing altogether and for the last thirty years of his life his only really major work was the choral piece *Stabat Mater*. Nobody is quite sure why. By then, though, he had racked up enormous success at home and abroad.

In 1816, when Rossini's opera *The Barber of Seville* – now one of the most performed operas in the world – was premiered, the audience booed and shouted the name 'Paisiello' over and over again. The reason? Paisiello had composed a version of the opera long before Rossini's and his was much more popular at the time. History changed all that though.

Rossini loved his food, so it seems appropriate that his name has been attached to more dishes than any other composer. As well as Tournedos Rossini, which is steak layered on croutons with foie gras and truffles on top, you will also find dishes such as Omelette Rossini and Salade Rossini.

Check it out

'Largo al factotum' from *The Barber of Seville* | Overture to *The Silken Ladder* | Overture to *The Thieving Magpie* | Overture to *William Tell*

Well I never!

Rossini claimed to have written the whole of *The Barber of Seville* in just thirteen days.

Namedrop

Isabella Colbran and Olympe Pélissier. Isabella was Rossini's soprano wife; Olympe was the mistress whom, when Isabella died, he married.

★ ★ ★

John RUTTER (born 1945)

John Rutter's music is probably performed more often and in more places around Britain than any other living British classical composer. Based in Cambridge, his choral anthems and carols have become a major part of church services in this country. His most famous work is his stunningly beautiful *Requiem*, which is often performed by amateur choral groups.

Check it out

A Gaelic Blessing, often referred to by mischievous choirboys as 'A Garlic Dressing' | *For the Beauty of the Earth* | *The Candlelight Carol*

★ ★ ★

Camille SAINT-SAËNS (1835–1921)

To say that Saint-Saëns was a clever kid is an understatement. This book is full of child stars, but he was probably the most prodigious of the lot. He could read and write and play tunes on the piano at the age of just two. By the age of seven he was something of an expert in lepidoptery (the study of insects, to us mere mortals). His best-known piece is *The Carnival of the Animals*, which he banned from being performed during his lifetime in case people stopped taking him seriously. The animal theme continues, albeit unwittingly, with his other famous work, his 'Organ' Symphony No. 3, which will forever be linked to 'sheep-pigs', after being used in the film *Babe*.

Check it out

Violin Sonata No. 1 in D minor | *Danse Macabre* | *Mon cœur s'ouvre à ta voix*, from his opera *Samson and Delilah* – a contender for most beautiful aria ever.

★ ★ ★

Erik SATIE (1866–1925)

This French composer is best known for his *Gymnopédies* Nos. 1 and 3 for piano. He was something of an eccentric and had a habit of giving many of his compositions ridiculous names.

His strangely titled pieces include: *Veritable Flabby Preludes (for a Dog)* | *Sketches and Exasperations of a Big Boob Made of Wood* | *Five Grins or Mona Lisa's Moustache* | *Menus for Childish Purposes* | *Three Pear-Shaped Pieces* | *Waltz of the Chocolate with Almonds*. He also wrote a remarkable piano piece called *Vexations* which is made of the same few bars of music which are played again and again and again – a total of 840 times.

Check it out

Three Gnossiennes | *Parade*, mad ballet music, perfect for putting on when you've come home merry after a night on the razz.

★ ★ ★

Franz SCHUBERT (1797–1828)

Some composers seem to find one thing and stick to it like glue. If Schubert is salt, then songs (or, as he would have said, Lieder) are pepper. Despite dying at the age of 31, he composed more than 600 of them. To be fair, he also found time for more or less nine symphonies (one was unfinished), eleven operas and around 400 other pieces. All of this was completed in a composing career that lasted for just 18 years. In 1815 alone he wrote 144 songs, including eight in one day in October, along with a symphony, two masses and assorted other works. He also liked to have fun and, in his day, he was famous for his musical parties known as Schubertiads.

Schubert stood at only 5'1" in his stockinged feet. This diminutive frame, added to his rather plump body, earned him the nickname 'Schwammerl' among his friends. This translates as 'the little mushroom'.

Check it out

Marche militaire No. 1 | Overture and Incidental Music to *Rosamunde* | Piano Quintet (*'Trout'*) based on one of his songs | Piano Sonata No. 21 | Symphony No. 8 (*'Unfinished'*)

Well I never!

Schubert was a notoriously bad timekeeper. His friends' letters are strewn with references to him being tardy or not showing up at all.

★ ★ ★

Robert SCHUMANN (1810–56)

Schumann was a great composer, but as a performer he lived in the shadow of his wife Clara, a renowned concert pianist. He suffered from syphilis and depression, and attempted suicide by throwing himself into the Rhine at the age of 44. Two years later, he died in an asylum.

Check it out

Scenes from Childhood No. 7 – Dreaming | *Fantasie in C* | Piano Concerto in A minor | the song cycle *Dichterliebe*

★ ★ ★

Howard SHORE (born 1946)

This Canadian film composer has soared in popularity following the release of his soundtrack to the film version of *The Lord of the Rings* in 2001. He has also written the music to the two sequels.

Check it out
Gangs of New York | *The Aviator* | *Panic Room*

★ ★ ★

Dmitri SHOSTAKOVICH (1906–75)

Among the greatest of 20th century composers, Shostakovich spent his entire life falling in and out of favour with the ruling Communist Party in Russia. Despite the pressure over what sort of music he should compose, he still managed to write a stack of hits. He was also one of the first great film composers – with many of his movie scores still being performed today.

Check it out
Jazz Suites Nos. 1 and *2* | *Romance* from *The Gadfly* | *The Assault on Beautiful Gorky* | Symphony No. 5 | Piano Concerto No. 2

Well I never!
Having come in for some stick with his previous works, Shostakovich subtitled his Fifth Symphony 'A Soviet Artist's Response to Just Criticism' and people have been arguing, ever since, if he meant it or not.

★ ★ ★

Jean SIBELIUS (1865–1957)

He may have looked like a rather grumpy Kojak, with his shaven head and lollipop, but in his native Finland he was a musical hero. Many of his best-loved works are heavily influenced by the folk music of his homeland. He liked to drink and to smoke and was diagnosed as suffering from throat cancer in his forties. The operations to remove the malignant growths were successful and he lived for another half a century. More than twenty years before he died, having made enough money to live comfortably, he simply stopped composing and retired. Oh, and we lied about the lollipop.

Karelia Suite | The Swan of Tuonela | Finlandia | Valse Triste | Violin Concerto | Symphony No. 2

The Vienna Philharmonic Orchestra. Sibelius was desperate to be a violin player as much as a composer and he auditioned with them in 1891. Sadly, he never made the grade, so had to settle for writing one of the greatest violin concertos in the world.

★ ★ ★

Bedřich SMETANA (1824–84)

Smetana ended up suffering from deafness, syphilis and ultimately going completely mad. Before then he made his name as the father of Czech musical nationalism. His most popular piece, *Vltava* from *Má Vlast* (My Homeland) is about the passage of the River Vltava to the sea. His other big hit is the overture to his opera *The Bartered Bride*.

Smetana, like a number of composers, went deaf in later life. In his String Quartet No. 1, the violin plays a long high note, which Smetana said was meant to sound like the whistling in his ears.

★ ★ ★

STRAUSS FAMILY

This is one of the great dynasties of classical music, something along the lines of what Kirk and Michael Douglas are to acting today. Johann Strauss Senior was born in 1804 and his son, Johann Strauss Junior, came into the world 19 years later. Johann Sr is known as the 'Father of the Waltz', having written 152 of them. Having said that, his most famous work is the infectiously fun *Radetzky March*, which isn't actually a waltz at all. He also had the top orchestra in Vienna. That was, until his son Johann Jr came along. He was the Bill Gates of classical music, turning music for dancing into big business and giving us a whole host of waltzes in the process, including the most popular of them all, *The Blue Danube*. He had six orchestras running simultaneously and wrote nearly 400 waltzes during his life. His brothers Josef and Eduard (each of whom had around 300 compositions to their names) both ended up conducting one of other of Johann Jr's orchestras.

Check it out

Die Fledermaus (The Bat), an operetta, jam-packed with great tunes, and written when Johann Jr was 51.

★ ★ ★

Richard STRAUSS (1864–1949)

No relation to the Viennese Strauss family, Richard Strauss is best known for *Also sprach Zarathustra*, which was used in the Stanley Kubrick film *2001: A Space Odyssey*. He is regarded as one of the last great German romantics despite the fact that he was writing on well into the 20th century. His international standing fell when he decided to continue working in Germany after 1939, although at the end of the Second World War he was acquitted of being a Nazi collaborator.

Strauss was extremely skilled in the then popular card game of 'Scat' and would often win huge amounts of money playing the game. On one occasion, he had fleeced so much from virtually all the Bayreuth Orchestra that they refused to go on and perform until Winifred Wagner, Richard Wagner's daughter-in-law, had reimbursed them.

Check it out

Der Rosenkavalier | Four Last Songs

Well I never!

Strauss was said to be henpecked by his wife, Pauline, a one-time soprano. When she got too much for him at one particular rehearsal, he got his revenge by shouting the last line of his opera, *Salome*: 'Kill that woman!'

★ ★ ★

Igor STRAVINSKY (1882–1971)

One of the great composers of the 20th century, this Russian caused a storm during his lifetime because of the innovative style of his music. As you can see for yourself later in this book, he's something of a rent-a-quote, having said some 'bon mot' about virtually every aspect of music at some point – a sort of Groucho Marx of classical music.

Check it out

The Rite of Spring, which literally caused a riot at its premiere | *The Firebird*, which has one of the best finales anywhere in classical music | the *Symphony in C*, if you're feeling adventurous, is one that really grows on you

Well I never!

Stravinsky was a big friend of Rimsky-Korsakov (as well being his pupil) and he wrote the music for RK's wedding

★ ★ ★

Joby TALBOT (born 1971)

Joby Talbot was named as Classic FM's first-ever Composer in Residence in a scheme supported by the PRS Foundation for the promotion of new music. He has composed a wide range of classical, pop and film music. He first came to prominence as a member of the pop group The Divine Comedy.

Check it out

The Dying Swan | *Robbie the Reindeer* | *The League of Gentlemen* | *The Hitchhiker's Guide to the Galaxy* | *Once Around the Sun*

★ ★ ★

John TAVENER (born 1944)

John Tavener's music reached its biggest-ever audience when his *Song for Athene* was used at the end of the funeral service held at Westminster Abbey for Diana, Princess of Wales. In the 1980s he wrote *The Protecting Veil* for the cellist Steven Isserlis and more recently found his choral piece *The Lamb* being used on TV to sell mobile phones.

Not to be confused with: John Taverner, with two 'r's, an English composer of sacred music born some 450 years earlier than John Tavener, one 'r'.

★ ★ ★

Peter TCHAIKOVSKY (1840–93)

One of the greatest of all composers, Tchaikovsky led a tortuous life. He suffered from depression and was suicidal on more than one occasion. He was driven to despair by the poor reception given to his early compositions (many of which are now huge hits) and by guilt over his homosexuality, which was socially unacceptable at the time. His benefactor throughout his life was a rich widow, who insisted they never actually meet. There is confusion over exactly how he died – officially, cholera from infected water claimed his life, although there is something evidence that he may have drunk it knowingly. Tchaikovsky had a knack for great tunes and lots of them. His ballets are among the most often performed today.

Check it out

The Nutcracker | 1812 Overture | Piano Concerto No. 1 | Symphony No. 6 ('Pathétique') | *Romeo and Juliet* | *Sleeping Beauty* | *Swan Lake*

Well I never!

When Tchaikovsky received his honorary degree from Cambridge University on 13th June, 1893, he was in amazing company. Also receiving degrees that day were Saint-Saëns, Max Bruch and Puccini's librettist, Arrigo Boito.

★ ★ ★

Jay UNGAR (born 1946)

This American composer became a star when a superb arrangement of his tune *The Ashokan Farewell* was played on Classic FM. There was a huge response from listeners to the piece, which was used as the theme to a television documentary called *The American Civil War*. It has now rocketed into the Top 10 of the annual Classic FM Hall of Fame listener vote. So far, Ungar resolutely remains a One-Hit-Wonder. It is of no relevance, whatsoever, that he shares his surname with the character played by Jack Lemmon in *The Odd Couple*.

★ ★ ★

Ralph VAUGHAN WILLIAMS (1872–1958)

The music of Ralph Vaughan Williams is as English as warm beer and cricket on the village green. Born in Gloucestershire, he collected traditional English folk songs from a young age and it's these tunes which went on to provide him with the core of many of his subsequent hits. He studied at the Royal College of Music in London, where he sat just a couple of desks along from another great British composer, one Gustav Holst. Since Classic FM began broadcasting in 1992, the popularity of Vaughan Williams has grown steadily each year.

Ralph Vaughan Williams wasn't the only famous name in his family – his great uncle was none other than Charles Darwin. By the way, 'Ralph', in this instance is pronounced to rhyme with 'safe', as in the actor Ralph Fiennes.

Check it out

Fantasia on a Theme of Thomas Tallis | *The Lark Ascending* | *English Folk Song Suite* | *Fantasia on Greensleeves* | Symphony No. 2 ('London')

Namedrop

Down Ampney, the name of the village in Gloucestershire where RVW was born and lived until he was two and a bit.

★ ★ ★

Giuseppe VERDI (1813–1901)

The fact that when we think of Italy, we think of opera is in no small part down to this mischievous-looking man, considered by many to be the greatest of all Italian opera composers. Big tuneful hits fill his 26 operas and the majority of them remain on the bill of fare at opera houses around the world today. When *Aida* received its premiere in Italy, the audience loved it so much that the standing ovation lasted for no fewer than 32 curtain calls. His other major work, the *Requiem*, is regarded as one of the greatest pieces of choral music ever written.

Check it out

'Celeste Aida' and *The Grand March* from *Aida* | Overture to *La forza del destino* | 'Questa o quella' and 'La donna è mobile' from *Rigoletto* | 'Sempre libera' from *La traviata* | *Anvil Chorus* from *Il trovatore* | *Chorus of the Hebrew Slaves* from *Nabucco* | 'Dies irae' from the *Requiem*

Well I never!

'Viva Verdi' was the most fashionable line of graffiti in the 1860s, found chalked on many an Italian wall. Italian nationalists were campaigning for the king, Victor Emmanuel, and the line stood for 'Viva **V**ictor **E**mmanuel, **R**e **D**'Italia' – Long live Victor Emmanuel, King of Italy. Great free publicity.

★ ★ ★

Antonio VIVALDI (1678–1741)

Despite the fact that Vivaldi wrote somewhere around 800 different works, his music was rarely played from his death in 1741 right through to the middle of the 20th century. He then had something of a comeback and now sits near the top of the list of most-performed baroque composers. Were there to be a 'Musical Redheads Hall of Fame', he'd be up there with Cilla Black and Mick Hucknall. Even though he was a priest, he used to tour with both a top soprano and her sister. Despite his denials, everyone thought that there was more to this threesome than just trio sonatas. And they say blondes have all the fun.

Check it out

Four Seasons | *Gloria* | *Nulla in mundo pax sincera*, used in the film *Shine*

Well I never!

Despite being born some 500 kilometres away on the other side of the Alps, Vivaldi ended up in the next graveyard along from Mozart in Vienna. Both of them were in paupers' graves.

★ ★ ★

Richard WAGNER (1813–83)

Think Wagner, think 'extreme'. His music extreme, and it tends to elicit extreme reactions from listeners. It's love or hate with him. People rarely use the word 'quite' in connection with Wagner. Despite this genius, he was a deeply flawed character – a racist, anti-Semitic, Machiavellian serial philanderer with a monstrous ego. Sound awful? Well, try the music before you make up your mind. His greatest achievement is the four operas that make up *The Ring Cycle*, which together last for more than 20 hours. No, that's not a misprint.

One of the stranger uses of Wagner's music came in the cartoon *What's Opera, Doc?* Bugs Bunny and his lifelong adversary Elmer Fudd can be heard singing along to parts of *Die Walküre* and *Tannhäuser*, giving many youngsters their first taste of opera.

Check it out

Overture to *The Flying Dutchman* | Prelude to Act 1 of *Lohengrin* | *Bridal Chorus* from *Lohengrin* | *Ride of the Valkyries* from *Die Walküre*, which was used as American helicopters swooped into Vietnam in the film *Apocalypse Now* | *Siegfried's Funeral March* from *Götterdämmerung* | *Pilgrims' Chorus* from *Tannhäuser* | Prelude to *Tristan and Isolde*

Namedrop

Siegfried Idyll, possibly the most special birthday present ever. Wagner wrote it for his new wife, Cosima. He smuggled a chamber orchestra of musicians onto the landing outside her bedroom in 1870 and had them play this new work for her. Definitely one better than breakfast in bed.

★ ★ ★

William WALTON (1902–83)

If Vaughan Williams' music can evoke a picture of pastoral England, then Walton is able to convey the majesty – the 'pomp' to Vaughan-Williams' 'circumstance'. Pieces such as *Crown Imperial* and *Orb and Sceptre* seem to be written in the key of ermine.

Check it out

Spitfire Prelude and Fugue | his *Henry V Suite*, written for Laurence Olivier's 1944 film

Charles-Marie WIDOR (1844–1937)

During his time, Widor (pronounced Vee Door) was the Thierry Henry of the organ world – a truly dazzling player. His Organ Symphony No. 5, and in particular the *Toccata* which ends it, has become a big part of many wedding ceremonies.

Namedrop

The Montgolfier Brothers, the balloon pioneers. Widor was vaguely related, on his mother's side.

★ ★ ★

John WILLIAMS (born 1932)

Arguably the greatest living film composer. If a movie has a John Williams soundtrack, it nearly always means that it's a Hollywood blockbuster. His hit list includes *Star Wars*, *Harry Potter*, *Schindler's List*, *Superman* and *E.T.*

Not to be confused with: the other John Williams, a brilliant classical guitarist.

The London Symphony Orchestra, with whom Williams has a long term relationship. They have recorded many of his soundtracks, including *Raiders of the Lost Ark*, *Superman* and all of the *Star Wars* movies.

★ ★ ★

Hans ZIMMER (born 1957)

Another movie composer, Hans Zimmer is known principally for his soundtrack to *Gladiator*, along with a string of other movie scores. He had early success as the writer of television theme tunes.

Mission Impossible | *The Last Samurai* | *Rain Man* | *Pearl Harbour*

★ ★ ★

Domenico ZIPOLI (1688–1726)

Until the premiere of Zimmer's *Gladiator*, this organist and composer's main job was to be the chief 'Z' in classical music. He hailed from Naples, but towards the end of his life he got the travel bug and emigrated to Argentina. His one surviving hit is *Elevazione*, which has become a big favourite for Classic FM listeners.

 Well I never!

In the 1970s, twenty-odd previously unknown works by Zipoli turned up in Bolivia (he had been a Jesuit missionary out in Paraguay).

★ ★ ★

Ten famous operas

– what's *actually* going on?

Mozart: THE MAGIC FLUTE
(*or* Papageno was a Rolling Stone)

It is often said that *The Magic Flute* is Mozart's version of a panto – silly, camp in places and with a great stage baddie to boo and hiss (the Queen of the Night). The plot is bizarre, too, even by opera standards.

THE PLOT

Act 1

Prince Tamino is knocked unconscious by a monster, which is then killed by three mysterious ladies, who quite fancy him. On waking, he meets a mischievous birdcatcher (is that really a job?) called Papageno. The Three Ladies (diddle-y-dit-di-dee) padlock Papageno's mouth for lying and show Tamino a picture of a beautiful girl, the daughter of the Queen. They tell him that she is a prisoner of nasty Zorastro and he decides he will free her. Scene change.

Pamina, the girl in the picture, is receiving the unwanted attentions of Zorastro's number two, Monastatos. Papageno sees him off, much to Pamina's delight. Scene change again.

Tamino tries to gain entry into three temples, but fails twice. At the third attempt, a speaker emerges and tells him that Zorastro is no baddie after all, but that the Queen of the Night is. Tamino sings and plays his magic flute (yes, THE magic flute) and soothes a few savage beasts in the process. He scarpers, stage right, though, when he hears Papageno's pan-pipe (NOT the magic flute).

In true panto style, Papageno enters stage left, with Pamina. When Monastatos enters and things look like turning ugly, Papageno plays his magic chimes (there's a lot of it about – magic, that is) and Monastatos dances off. Zorastro now enters, amidst huge pomp. Pamina and Papageno explain what had been going on so, when Monastatos arrives, dragging our hero Tamino, he gets short shrift and is sent off, with his ear now home to flea. Oh, and a good flogging. (Well, this is before the corporal punishment ban.) Zorastro also asks Papageno and Tamino to prove themselves. Exciting. End of Act 1. Time for a Chunky Choc Ice.

Act 2

Tamino and Papageno's ordeals kick off. They are left alone, but who should show up but the Three Ladies (diddle-y-dit-di-dee), who try to persuade them to give it all up and nip off for a cheeky capuccino. Both stay shtumm, and, so, Zorastro appears to tell them they have passed test number one. Scene change.

Pamina is asleep. The sleazy Monastatos slimes up to her, intent on who knows what, but is forced back by the Queen of the Night – he must be getting used to this by now. The evil Queen slings Pam a dagger and asks her to kill Zorastro. Slimeball Monastatos slithers up to Pam, again, and says he'll tell all – about the dagger – to Zorastro, if she doesn't … you know! Zorastro arrives not a moment too soon and dispatches Monastatos – now with veritable colony of insects in his aural canal. Scene change.

Papageno meets his future love, Papagena, who is, shall we say, mature in years and displeasing of fizzog. Papageno is not exactly impressed. Meanwhile, Pamina has hooked up with Tamino, but he's still on his sponsored silence and she's heartbroken that he won't speak to her. Zorastro appears to tell Pam and Tam to say what could be their final goodbye. Papageno is forced to swear undying love to the somewhat facially challenged crone. When he does – PUFF! – she's transformed into the young and beautiful Papagena, although they can't be together until Pap has proved himself.

Tamino is then led off for his final ordeals – fire and water. With Pamina in tow, he passes with flying colours, dropping only a few points for not using his mirror. Papageno is also cheered up when he is allowed to be with Papagena. Just to round things off, Zorastro vanquishes the Queen of the Night and her Three Ladies (diddle-y-dit-di-dee) in a huge flood of bright, do-gooding light. All are happy, the opera is over and it's time to join the mad rush to get your coat from the cloakroom.

Verdi: LA TRAVIATA
(*or* TB or not TB)

Verdi got the plot of his opera from a play written by Alexandre Dumas *fils*, the son of the guy who wrote *The Three Musketeers*. It's a great love story, set in Paris, with the only real baddie being Tuberculosis.

THE PLOT

Act 1

There's a party going on, thrown by our heroine, Violetta, a good-time girl of the Paris party scene, who is, by the time we meet her, already ill. Her friend, Gastone, tells her that 'my mate fancies you' – my mate being Alfredo. Alfredo then leads the assembled partygoers in a great drinking song after which he stays to talk to Violetta. He tells her he loves her and she, more or less, tells him she loves him. When everybody else has left, though, Violetta sings to herself about her new love, while at the same time telling herself to deny it. Short act, act one. Only time for a quick Oyster Shell.

Act 2

Time has clearly passed. Violetta and Alfredo are living together (in sin) in the country. All is well, apart from the fact that Alfie finds out that Vi has been selling her jewellery to pay the bills. Just as she receives a party invite to Paris, he decides to go off to the capital to raise money.

A guest is announced. It is Alfredo's father, Georgio. He asks her to give his son up, so that no whiff of scandal can attach itself to his family, especially as he's got his daughter's wedding coming up. As the two discuss the affair, each gradually grows on the other – the father sees her as not a gold-digger after all, and she sees his point so much that she agrees to give up her love. She writes Alfie a note, but he enters, so she hides it. She says goodbye. After she's gone, he is handed her letter – which says 'I've gone back to my old life, to be a kept woman of Baron Douphol's' – and, despite a word from his Dad, he rushes off to Paris. Scene change.

At the party of Violetta's friend, Flora, Alfredo enters and, not far behind him, Baron Douphol, with Violetta on his arm. Alfredo insults Violetta in front of everyone, the Baron challenges him and Violetta faints. Dramatic stuff. When she recovers, she sings of her love for Alfredo. End of Act 2. Time for a Vanilla tub with its own spoon in the lid.

Act 3

Time has clearly passed, again. Violetta is on her deathbed. She wakes from her stupor to re-read a letter from Alfredo's Dad, telling her that the Baron was wounded in the duel and, more importantly, that Alfredo knows that she was forced to give him up. Oh, and PS, he's on his way to see her. She talks of death, just before Alfie enters. He tells her he'll take her off to Paris and all will be ok. She'd love to believe him but, as Alfie looks on, she dies. Very sad. Cue the Kleenex.

Rossini: THE BARBER OF SEVILLE
(*or* Something for the Weak End)

Rossini took a bit of risk setting his own version of the Barber of Seville story, mainly because there already existed a version by the composer Paisiello. Back then, Paisiello was far more popular than Rossini. The gamble paid off though. So much so that, today, Rossini's name is almost synonymous with opera, whereas Paisiello's is usually followed by the word 'Who?'.

THE PLOT

Act 1

Dr Bartolo has a ward, the young and beautiful Rosina. Count Almaviva fancies Rosina, but Bartolo keeps a watchful eye on her. Almaviva gets his servant, Fiorello, to serenade her with musicians. Amidst the general cacophony of musicians, Figaro enters. Figaro is Dr Bartolo's barber. Of course he is. Who else would he be? He announces himself in one of the most famous arias ever (the 'Figaro, Figaro, Figaro, Figaro ...' one).

Rosina has noticed Almaviva, though, and drops a letter from her balcony asking him his name. He tells her it is Lindoro (thus obeying opera rule number one – 'Never use your real name if a false one could be more confusing'). Meanwhile, as Dr Bartolo tells his singing teacher that he suspects Almaviva of being after his ward, Figaro manages to let Rosina know that his 'cousin Lindoro' (Almaviva, yes? Are you keeping up?) is crazy about her. Dr Bartolo lectures her on dropping letters from the balcony and about what will happen if she crosses him.

Meanwhile, Lindoro (the artist formerly known as Almaviva) gets into Rosina's house disguised as, wait for it ... a tipsy soldier. What else? He then claims the right to be billeted there. Genius. He makes himself known to Rosina and refuses to take a blind bit of notice of Rosina's governess, of the singing teacher or even of the police, who arrive in a scene more reminiscent of the great

Keystone Cops than the great composers. General mayhem ensues. Interval. Time for a Screwball.

Act 2

Almaviva, aka Lindoro aka Tipsy Soldier, is now dressed up as Don Alonso, a new music teacher, supposedly sent by Bartolo's own music teacher, who he says is ill. He tells Bartolo that he has a letter from Almaviva (himself) and says he will persuade Rosina that it was given to him by one of Almaviva's (that's himself) many mistresses, thus making Almaviva (himself, remember) look bad. Figaro then enters, wanting to shave Bartolo. Well, he is a barber. Bartolo says no, but Figaro insists, creates a bit of a diversion and manages to get Almaviva (aka Lindoro aka Tipsy Soldier aka Don Alonso) and Rosina together for a few moments. Cue the real music teacher, who is not ill. Damn. Almaviva (aka … etc) and Figaro persuade him that he IS ill, and should go home. Figaro then shaves Bartolo, while Almaviva and Rosina secretly – but not secretly enough – plan to run away together. I say 'not secretly enough' because, of course, Bartolo overhears them. When he has sent Almaviva packing, Bartolo shows Rosina the letter from Almaviva, telling her it's from one of his mistresses. Slightly naffed off, Rosina spills her guts to Bartolo about the planned elopement, and agrees to marry Bartolo.

But suddenly, out of nowhere, a storm blows up. Figaro and Almaviva show up and, of course, Al and Ros make up. Figaro has planned their escape with a ladder to the balcony. When the ladder disappears, though, Figaro realises that they've been rumbled. But, as luck would have it, the deus ex machina turns up in the form of … a notary. Of course. Who else would show up just then but someone who is able to marry people? In fact, he was there to marry Bartolo and Rosina, but instead marries Almaviva and Rosina. In the end, everyone comes round to the idea – even Bartolo, who is offered money by Almaviva as a compensation for Rosina's dowry. Love, or at least a mixture of love and money, changes everything.

Wagner: TRISTAN UND ISOLDE

(*or* I'd like to know where … you got the potion)

This is one of the shorter Wagner operas, weighing in at just a little over three and a half hours, as opposed to, say, the *Ring* cycle of operas, which take around 20 hours to perform. Indeed, several people have been 'lost' inside a *Ring* cycle, having entered but never made it out – never seen again. Police say there is very little they can do other than keep an open mind.

THE PLOT

Act 1

Tristan is on his way back from Ireland to Cornwall. We know, we know – not the classic romantic setting one thinks of for an opera, but bear with us. With him, he had Isolde, who he loves, but whom he is taking back to marry his Uncle Mark, the King of Cornwall. When Isolde finds out that she is intended for Mark and not Tristan, she gets more than a little annoyed, invoking the elements to come to destroy the ship and all who sail in it. Isolde sends for Tristan and asks her Lady-in-Waiting to make up a death potion that she will give him to drink. Tristan arrives and Isolde proposes a toast 'to us!'. Tristan drinks it, but, unknown to Isolde, her lady-in-waiting has substituted a love potion for the death potion. They sink into each others' arms. People crowd the deck and, amidst general jubilation, the Lady-in-Waiting tells them to get a room. Uh-oh, what will they tell King Mark? End of Act 1. Time for a Strawberry Mivvy.

Act 2

Everyone's gone out for a hunt with King Mark, Tristan included. Isolde signals Tristan to come to her by putting out a lighted torch. Tristan arrives and they rush into each other's arms. They (ahem …) bed down for a night of lurve, hoping the dawn will never come. Despite warnings from the Lady-in-Waiting that the night will soon be over, they carry on (ahem …) loving, singing their song of yearning for death through love – the *Liebestod*. Dawn arrives and with it the the King's party. The King is philosophical, if livid. The knight Melot wounds Tristan in the ensuing kerfuffle. End of Act 2. Time for a Mint Feast in the bar.

Act 3

Tristan is at his castle in Brittany – again, not the most romantic of settings, but still. He is wounded and lapsing in and out of conciousness. A shepherd is piping, keeping watch for the ship that will bring Isolde to heal his wounds. Tristan drifts through memories of Isolde, and how she healed his wounds before, back in Ireland. Suddenly, the piper pipes a jollier, sort of 'I can see Isolde's ship' type tune, and Tristan struggles to get up. In his eagerness, he tears the bandages from his wounds, and, when Isolde rushes in, he can only whisper her name before dying in her arms. Another ship docks – bearing King Mark *et al*. Tristan's faithful friend, Kurwenal, thinks they've come after Isolde and so goes for them, killing Melot, the guy who wounded Tristan. The Lady-in-Waiting, though, rushes in to say that she had confessed to the king about switching the death potion with the love potion, but Isolde doesn't care. She sings her *Liebestod*, and, staring at the body of her lover, falls upon him, dead. Strong stuff. You may need a small sharpener yourself.

★ ★ ★

Puccini: LA BOHÈME
(*or* **Do Re Mimi**)

If you haven't ever seen an opera, *La Bohème*'s not a bad place to start. It's a slushy, Sunday afternoon movie with music. If you cried your head off at *An Affair to Remember*, then this is the opera for you.

THE PLOT

Act 1

Rodolfo, the lead, is living in an arty student flat. He's a writer and his flatmates include a painter and a musician. It's Christmas Eve 1830, and they are so broke that Rodolfo has to use the article that he is writing to keep the fire going. Schaunard, the musical flatmate, arrives home with money, and takes everyone out for supper. Rodolfo stays in, to try to write. There's a knock at the door. It's Mimi, who asks him for a light for her candle, which has blown out leaving her in the dark – yeah, right. She has a brief coughing fit, drops her key and they both end up looking for it. Their hands meet and ... VOOM! Or should I say, his hand meets her tiny frozen hand and ... VOOM! She tells him she's an embroiderer – how romantic. Rodolfo's friends call him to come for supper but he decides to stay and sing songs about Mimi in the moonlight. End of Act 1. Time for a pre-plated prawn sandwich in the bar.

Act 2

Mimi meets everyone. She is introduced to Rodolfo's friends, particularly Marcello (the artist) and Musetta, who fancies Marcello. Musetta does a saucy little slow waltz for Marcello and they cuddle. Everything is going well, apart from the bill for supper, which Musetta manages to get charged to one of her other suitors. End of Act 2. Pan-fried kettle chips in foyer.

Act 3

Time has passed. Mimi tells Marcello that Rodolfo is a bit clingy and jealous and she thinks she might dump him. She has another coughing fit. (Either Puccini is trying to tell us something, or he can even see music in an inflamed oesophagus.) Rodolfo enters and, indeed, he acts jealous and clingy. Although he suspects she might be unwell, they decide to split up. Meanwhile Marcello gets a little miffed at Musetta flirting. Blimey, it's like an episode of *Desperate Housewives*. End of Act 3. Glass of pinot grigio in the crush bar.

Act 4

Back in the flat. Rodolfo is missing Mimi and Marcello is missing Musetta. The whole thing has the air of a student bedsit, minus the reruns of *Bargain Hunt*. Musetta bursts in, frantic. She had found Mimi at the bottom of the stairs, collapsed. Rodolfo rushes off and carries her into the flat. They lay her on the bed and she seems a little better, but very weak. Musetta decides to sell her earrings to raise money for medicine and one of the other flatmates decide to sell his coat. (Possibly the only place in opera where someone sings goodbye to a coat. True, honest.) Alone, Mimi and Rodolfo think about happier times together. The others come back and try to help Mimi, but she dies. At first, Rodolfo – at the other side of the room – doesn't realise, but then he works out the looks on the others' faces and just explodes in grief, shout/singing 'Mimi!' before the curtain closes. What an ending.

★ ★ ★

Bizet: CARMEN
(*or* Smoke Gets in Your Arias)

Poor Bizet. He died before *Carmen* had become a hit. And it wasn't as if it happened hundreds of years later. When he died, it was flopping, nightly. Then, for some reason, a mere handful of performances later, it was being hailed as sensational. Now, it's probably the most performed opera in the world.

THE PLOT

Act 1

It's Seville 1830, and boy, is it hot. It's hot outside in the town square, and it's even hotter inside the factory, where the gypsy Carmen and her co-workers make cigarettes all day long. A bunch of soldiers parade across the square. One of them, a corporal called José, tells his lieutenant that the girls in the factory are quite pretty. The factory hooter goes and the largely male crowd watch the parade of girls go past. The girls, for their part, sing beautiful songs … about cigarettes. No lie. (There is no truth in the rumour that Bizet was originally going to call this opera *The Silk Cut Ladder* or *Tales from the Vienna Woodbines*.)

Carmen leaves the factory and sings her saucy Habañera (a Spanish dance with words). She's positively 'smokin''. She throws a flower at José, the corporal, and then runs off. José talks to his foster-sister, Micaela, about his mum and about money. Supposedly, José fancies Micaela, but it sure doesn't feel like it.

Suddenly, there's a bit of a fuss coming from the cigarette factory. Someone's been stabbed and the word is it was Carmen who did the deed. José goes into the factory and brings Carmen out. The lieutenant starts to make out her arrest warrant but José, instead of handcuffing her, lets her go, clearly in love with her. End of Act 1 – time for that tuna salad which you brought from home in a Tupperware box to avoid paying opera house prices.

Act 2

We're in a tavern. Carmen and her two gypsy friends are singing. The matador Escamillo walks in and quite obviously has the hots for Carmen. She's not interested, though. Neither is she interested in the lieutenant, who tries his luck as well. Gosh, this woman is beating them off with a stick! Turns out, she does want José, after all. He was jailed over the cigarette factory incident, although he's being released from prison today. Suddenly, the pub shuts and smugglers appear from nowhere. Fantastic – a lock-in. Carmen cries off the smuggling that night, in favour of seducing José. In fact, when he arrives, they get straight down to unfinished business. Sadly, a bugle sounds, which tells him he needs to get back and join the anti-smuggling party. Carmen tries to exert her feminine wiles on him, and, when this fails, resorts to feminine badgering. No need, though, because the lieutenant suddenly walks in. Ah! Tricky one, this. José feels he has no choice but to defend Carmen and fights the lieutenant. Cue the smugglers, who could smell a fight a mile away, and they join in. Oh dear. Looks like José has just left the army and become a smuggler. His family wouldn't consider it a great career move. End of Act 2 – have a word with the commissionaire and nip out for a cheeky pint at the pub just up the road. (That's The Kemble's Head (near the Royal Opera House) or The Welsh Harp (near the Coliseum).)

.

Act 3

We're out in the wilds with José, Carmen and the smugglers. José is having the biggest 'what have I done?' moment of his life. Carmen is rapidly going off him. Together with her gypsy girlfriends, she reads her own fortune – you know, just to cheer herself up, because there's never any death in these things, is there? Oh, what's this? Death! What a surprise, Carmen believes it 100%, always having been one for fate. The smugglers and the girls, Carmen included, go off for a quick smuggle and José is left on watch. Micaela, his foster sister, comes looking for him, as does Escamillo, the matador. He says he loves Carmen and the two blokes fight. José is winning on points when the smugglers and the girls return. Carmen and Escamillo flash each other one of those 'play your cards right' looks, and he ends up inviting the whole party back to his gaffe in Seville. Micaela suddenly shows herself and begs José to come back to his poor dying mum. Timing, or what, Mum! What will happen? Act 3 will end, that's what will happen. Time for a … well, as it's *Carmen*, a nifty cig, stood outside the opera house door.

Act 4

We're in the Bull Ring – Seville, not Birmingham – and this is where it's all going to happen. Escamillo has got his tight trousers and silly hat on, and is strutting his stuff. Carmen is there with Escamillo, all loved up. Her gypsy girlfriends tell her that José is in the crowd, somewhere and he's tooled up. She spies him and goes to talk. They argue over the noise of the crowd and the whole opera climaxes with Carmen throwing her ring at him, and, as the crowd erupts at Escamillo's win over the bull, José stabs Carmen. The crowd close in on him and the curtain closes. So after all that, it wasn't the cigarettes that killed her.

★ ★ ★

Mascagni: CAVALLERIA RUSTICANA
(*or* Verismo Greater Love)

Mascagni's only real big hit, *Cavalleria Rusticana*, made its composer a fortune, but it was, by all accounts, a fortune that he lost again. It's often called the start of what is known as 'verismo' opera – real life opera, or if you like, even, soap opera. Verismo composers – Puccini was another – always took subjects that were gritty and 'of their day'. Mascagni's was based on a book by Verga that would have certainly raised eyebrows with its audience with its themes of infidelity and pregnancy. It won Mascagni a prize for the best one-act opera in 1889. As a result, of course, there's no interval, so you'll have to take a snack in your pocket and eat it while nobody's looking. Chocolate is a bad idea and so are crisps.

THE PLOT

It's Easter, in a Sicilian village. Santuzza, a young girl, doorsteps Mamma Lucia and asks her about her son, Turiddu. He's gone off to another village to get wine, she is told. But someone saw him in the village, during the night. Mamma Lucia says she'd better come inside. What Santuzza is not telling Mamma Lucia is that she is pregnant.

Alfio plods in, with his horse and cart. He is the village carter and, just to prove it, sings a jolly little song about how lovely it is to be a village carter. It also mentions how lovely it is being married to Lola. (There is no truth in the rumour that Mascagni deleted the lines *'Le sue labbra erano come la cola di ciliegia'* – or 'her lips were like cherry cola'.) Alfio asks Mamma Lucia for wine, but is told Turiddu has gone for off for more. Alfio, too, says he saw Turiddu not far from his house, this morning. Mmm. Curiouser and curiouser. Santuzza and Mamma Lucia exchange glances. Alfio goes off on his way, and Santuzza leads everyone in the Easter Hymn. No sign of eggs, though. Then after badgering from Mamma Lucia, she spills her guts and explains what's been going on. Turiddu had loved Lola, but then he went off to war. Lola married Alfio. When

Turridu came back from the war, he started seeing Santuzza. She fell pregnant, but he still loves Lola and sees her whenever Alfio is off 'carting'.

Turridu enters. Santuzza has a go at him for saying he was off buying wine when he was actually off with Lola. Turridu says he will be toast if Alfio finds out, and Santuzza is then a bit scared for him. Sadly, despite it all, she doesn't want to lose him. Lola comes by, and sings her way into church. Turridu, despite Santuzza's best begging efforts, follows her in, but not before Santuzza has cursed him. When Alfio comes in, then, Santuzza is more than happy to spill the beans about what's been going on.

> At this point, there's an 'intermezzo' – literally, a bit stuck in.
> In the case of *Cavalleria Rusticana*, it's probably the most
> famous 'bit stuck in' in opera history, and is one of the keys
> to the opera's success. It is, quite simply, a fantastic tune.

When the congregation come out of church, Turridu is on a high, with Lola by his side. They go off, with friends, to drink wine in Mamma Luccia's trattoria. They drink wine and sing about drinking wine, until Alfio appears. Things get tense and Alfio confronts Turridu. The challenge takes the traditional Sicilian form of an embrace, with Turridu biting Alfio's ear. Don't ask. Smacks of Mike Tyson, but it's apparently a way of saying 'OK, I accept your challenge' in Sicilian.

Turridu goes to see his mum and tells her he's going away and might be some time. If he doesn't come back, in fact, could she look after Santuzza? He leaves just as Santuzza enters, with lots of people from the village. They are all comforting each other when, in a piercing scream, someone yells from outside that Turridu has been murdered. Santuzza faints, and the curtain comes down.

Donizetti: THE ELIXIR OF LOVE
(*or* Finding Nemorino)

Donizetti was Mr Opera in the first half of the 19th century. He wrote his first opera at the age of 21 and then continued at a rate of just over three operas every year after that, until forced to stop by paralysis at the age of 48.

The Elixir of Love was written in less than two weeks, when the manager of the Teatro della Canobbiana in Milan begged Donizetti to help him out. The composer of his scheduled opera had let him down and he suggested that Donizetti might just nip and tuck an old one. Suitably challenged, Donizetti and his words man, Romani, set to work and produced one of his most loved operas in a fortnight. If this was Wagner, that would be the length of the opera.

THE PLOT

Act 1

First thing to say is we're in the countryside. Adina is the love interest in this opera and we're outside her farm. Nemorino, a village peasant, is sitting watching her read, all the while bemoaning the fact that she could never love a lowly idiot like him. Adina looks up from her book and laughs. She tells her friends she's reading the story of Tristan and Isolde, and says that Tristan won his love by giving her a magic love potion, which meant she couldn't keep her hands off him. Nemorino likes the sound of this potion. Some soldiers enter. The sergeant, Belcore, gives Adina a bunch of flowers and asks her to marry him. Adina is chuffed but turns him down. Nemorino, still looking on (these days it would be called stalking) wishes he had Belcore's courage to just go up to someone and propose.

When they are alone, Nemorino tries to pour out his feelings. Adina says she is just too flighty to be any use to him. In the village square, a travelling salesman has arrived. He's one of those quack doctors offering slightly dodgy cures for everything. Nemorino asks him for Isolde's Love Potion, please. The doctor, who's called Dulcamara, sees him coming. Dulcamara sells Nemorino a flask of wine, telling him it's a brilliant love potion that will work by the next day. Nemorino downs the whole 'potion' and is soon steaming drunk. As a result, not only is he loud and laddish, he's also not particularly bothered about Adina. His couldn't-care-less attitude annoys her because she's not used to being ignored. When Belcore comes in, she agrees to marry him. And within six days, too (he's being posted somewhere else and wants to wed before he goes). Still miffed that Nemorino is ignoring her, she even agrees to marry Belcore today. Nemorino is gobsmacked and begs her to just to wait one day, thinking his 'potion' will kick in. Belcore tells him to lay off and then he and Adina head off to see the notary. How depressed is Nemorino? He decides he needs some expert help – Dr Dulcamara! End of Act 1, time for warm Kia-Ora and Sunkist popcorn.

Act 2

Adina and Belcore's wedding banquet – but, don't worry, they haven't signed on the dotted line yet. They've just decided to get on with the party until the notary arrives. The bride and groom-to-be sing songs to each other. Meanwhile, Nemorino asks Dulcamara to help him, and is told that only more elixir can do the trick. But Nemorino is completely broke. Belcore then persuades Nemorino that, if he signs up to the army, he'll get twenty scudi. Nemorino signs the forms and runs off to find Dulcamara.

While he's away, news arrives that Nemorino's uncle has died, leaving him all his money. Although he doesn't know it, Nemorino is now a bit of a hot property, top of the list of eligible bachelors. As a result, when Nemorino returns, with yet more wine/potion down him, the girls flock round him like flies. Of course, he thinks it's the potion. Adina walks in and is more than a little miffed to find everyone suddenly loves Nemorino. She also tries to tell him that he shouldn't have joined the army, but he is dragged off by one of a bunch of eager women suitors. Dulcamara explains to Adina that he sold him a 'potion' – and offers to sell her one. It is at this point that Nemorino returns and sees Adina, with a tear in her eye. He realises that she must love him, after all. (The aria that goes with this, *'Una furtiva lagrima'*, is one of the most beautiful tenor arias ever.)

Adina buys Nemorino out of the army, and then admits to him that she loves him. Belcore is only slightly miffed, showing what sort he was all along. Dulcamara tries to claim that, as Nemorino is now rich, he can add 'wealth' to the long list of benefits of his love potion. All his wine/potion sells like hot cakes and he rides off into the sunset.

Beethoven: FIDELIO
(*or* Jailhouse Rocco)

It has been said that Beethoven was not particularly a fan of opera, writing only this one. He did try to make up for this by writing far too many overtures for it, though – four, in the end. Beethoven revised it quite a few times after the first version flopped, and it now stands at only two acts rather than the original three. He did think about venturing out on another opera, even writing the odd sketch for his own version of *Macbeth*. But in the end, this was to be his one and only.

It's all about Leonore, whose husband, Florestan, has disappeared. He worked for the State Department, and no one will believe Leonore when she says she smells a rat. She has narrowed her search to a jail near Seville. She gets a job in the prison, disguised as a man. You see? The opera's not even begun yet, and, already, it's a cock and bull story.

THE PLOT

Act 1

We're in a prison courtyard. Jaquino is the jailer's assistant and Marzelline is the jailer's daughter. Jaquino loves Marzelline, but – and this could be problematic – Marzelline loves the jailer's new assistant, Fidelio. Of course, as we know, Fidelio is a girl. Rocco, the jailer, comes in and they all sing in a quartet. Rocco then waxes lyrical on the subject of money, how lovely it is and how he'd like lots of it. Fidelio (or should we say Leonore) offers to do lots of his dirty work for him, and Rocco says how great he thinks he (she) is.

The prison governor, Pizarro, arrives and tells Rocco that the Minister of State, Don Fernando, is coming to check up on the prison. Pizarro says that Rocco should do away with ... you know who – Prisoner X! Rocco doesn't really want to. Pizarro says he'll do it himself. Fidelio (Leonore) hears all this and is more than a little incensed. She has big plans for a rescue attempt. She persuades

Rocco to allow the prisoners out into the open air, because it's the King's birthday. She eagerly watches their faces to see if her husband, Florestan, is amongst them. He isn't. Fidelio (Leonore) then gathers that she has to help Rocco dig a grave in the dungeon cell. It could be her husband's cell. She could save him! Or if not, she could jump in the grave with him, and die together. This thought cheers her up no end. End of Act 1 – time for an expensive tin of travel sweets and a coffee with plastic pot of chemical creamer.

Act 2

As the music descends, so do we ... into the dungeon. Florestan is indeed there, in chains. He's a bit worse for wear, as you can imagine, and, apart from anything else, is seeing visions of his gorgeous Leonore. Rocco and Fidelio (Leonore) come down to his dungeon. Fidelio (Leonore) gives him a drink and a little bit of food. Naturally, he's quite grateful. Cue Pizarro, who pulls out his dagger and moves to kill Florestan. Fidelio (Leonore) rushes to stand between them, revealing herself as Leonore (not literally, of course). A fanfare above tells them that the Minister of State has arrived. Pizarro has missed his moment and the game is up. All the prisoners are freed, the Minister of State recognises Florestan and orders Leonore to set him free, and Pizarro is arrested. Large ones all round.

Britten: PETER GRIMES
(*or* **Little Britten**)

Britten's *Peter Grimes* is both of those things – very modern and a real classic. It deals with Britten's favourite theme of the outsider in a small community. Interspersed throughout the opera are the gorgeous *Sea Interludes*, which have become a firm favourite on Classic FM.

THE PLOT

The Prologue

We're in the parish hall of an East Coast fishing village, in around 1830. The opera opens on an inquest into the death, at sea, of Peter Grimes's apprentice. The villagers suspect Grimes, but he explains that the wind blew them off course for three days and the boy died of exposure. The coroner believes Grimes but tells him he should not take another boy out – he should find himself a grown up. No one wants to really hear Grimes's version of events, but he does find some sort of kindred spirit in Ellen Orford, the schoolteacher. That's the end of the prologue.

Act 1

We are down by the boats. Ned Keene tells Peter he has found him another boy apprentice, who just needs fetching from the workhouse. The villagers refuse to have anything to do with the whole affair, but Ellen speaks up for Peter. Someone spies a storm at sea and they all hope that the sea will not be too cruel. A local captain, Balstrode, tells Grimes he's best off leaving the gossip of the village behind, but Peter says his roots are here. He tells Balstrode of the days at sea, with only the apprentice's corpse for company. He also muses how lovely life would be if Ellen were to become his wife. Gosh, he doesn't waste time, does he?

In the warm and cosy pub that night, all local life is there: the old lady, waiting for her laudanum from the chemist; the drunk, Bob Boles, making unwanted advances towards her nieces. Each time the door opens, the elements burst in.

When Peter arrives, things get a little tense. Ned Keene gets everyone doing some community singing, to distract them. Hobson and the new apprentice arrive and Peter leads him off home. The crowd all say 'Home? You call that home?' End of Act 1 – time for a tub of cockles and vinegar.

Act 2

It's a Sunday morning. Ellen is talking to John, Peter's new apprentice, about the relative merits of the workhouse over teaching. Or is it the other way round? She's worried to find his coat torn and his neck bruised. Peter comes in to take the boy off to work, despite it being a Sunday. Ellen and Peter quarrel, and he storms off with the boy, leaving Ellen to go home crying. When the congregation come out of the nearby church, some have heard the quarrelling and put two and two together. They ask Ellen to say what happened and get the impression that Peter is intent on murder. The men march off to Peter's beach hut. Before they get there, we see Peter in the hut with his new apprentice. He's still going on about how great life would have been if he'd been with Ellen. Then he hears the crowd approaching. He presumes they're coming to get the boy, and tries to hide him, bundling him down the cliff. The boy falls to his death with a bloodcurdling scream, and Peter climbs down after him. To lose one apprentice is unfortunate, but to lose two is careless. End of Act 2 – crabsticks with one thousand island dressing.

Act 3

There's a dance in the village hall. All the usual suspects are there. One of them tries to enlist support for the notion of going after Peter Grimes and charging him with murder. Ellen and Balstrode discuss the fact that Peter is nowhere to be seen. They have, however, found John the apprentice's yellow jersey washed up on the beach. Ah! Balstrode still thinks they might be able to help Peter.

Meanwhile, a posse of baying locals are gathered together to find Grimes. The search party can be heard shouting his name around the place, interspersed with the sound of the foghorn. Grimes is there, madly rambling on about home and all that has happened. Ellen and Balstrode find him and tell him they've come to take him home. Peter, ever so slightly wobbly, continues to ramble. Balstrode decides there's nothing they can do and tells him to take his boat out to sea and sink it. He comforts Ellen and leads her off.

Next morning in the village, the coastguard's report says that a boat has been seen out at sea, sinking. No one is particularly bothered. They carry on with their day.

Liszts

WHO FOLLOWED WHOM?

Hildegard of Bingen	1098–1179
Thomas Tallis	1505–1585
Giovanni da Palestrina	1525–1594
William Byrd	1537–1623
Claudio Monteverdi	1567–1643
Gregorio Allegri	1582–1652
Johann Pachelbel	1653–1706
Henry Purcell	1659–1695
Tomaso Albinoni	1671–1750
Antonio Vivaldi	1678–1741
Johann Sebastian Bach	1685–1750
George Frideric Handel	1685–1759
Joseph Haydn	1732–1809
Luigi Boccherini	1743–1805
Wolfgang Amadeus Mozart	1756–1791
Ludwig van Beethoven	1770–1827
Gioachino Rossini	1792–1868
Franz Schubert	1797–1828
Hector Berlioz	1803–1869
Johann Strauss senior	1804–1849
Felix Mendelssohn	1809–1847
Frédéric Chopin	1810–1849
Robert Schumann	1810–1856
Franz Liszt	1811–1886
Giuseppe Verdi	1813–1901
Richard Wagner	1813–1883
Jacques Offenbach	1819–1880
César Franck	1822–1890

Bedřich Smetana	1824–1884
Johann Strauss Jr	1825–1899
Alexander Borodin	1833–1887
Johannes Brahms	1833–1897
Camille Saint-Saëns	1835–1921
Léo Delibes	1836–1891
Georges Bizet	1838–1875
Max Bruch	1838–1920
Modest Moussorgsky	1838–1881
Peter Tchaikovsky	1840–1893
Antonín Dvořák	1841–1904
Jules Massenet	1842–1912
Edvard Grieg	1843–1907
Nikolai Rimsky-Korsakov	1844–1908
Gabriel Fauré	1845–1924
Edward Elgar	1857–1934
Gustav Mahler	1860–1911
Claude Debussy	1862–1918
Frederick Delius	1862–1934
Pietro Mascagni	1863–1945
Richard Strauss	1864–1949
Erik Satie	1866–1925
Ralph Vaughan Williams	1872–1958
Serge Rachmaninoff	1873–1943
Gustav Holst	1874–1934
Maurice Ravel	1875–1937
Igor Stravinsky	1882–1971
Serge Prokofieff	1891–1953
Carl Orff	1895–1982
George Gershwin	1898–1937
Aaron Copland	1900–1990
Joaquín Rodrigo	1901–1999
William Walton	1902–1983

Aram Khachaturian	1903–1978
Dmitri Shostakovich	1906–1975
Samuel Barber	1910–1981
Benjamin Britten	1913–1976
Leonard Bernstein	1918–1990
Malcolm Arnold	1921–
Henryk Górecki	1933–
Peter Maxwell Davies	1934–
Arvo Pärt	1935–
Philip Glass	1937–
Michael Nyman	1944–
John Tavener	1944–

TEN CLASSICS USED IN TV ADVERTS

Bach: *Air on the G String* – Hamlet Cigars
Delibes: Flower Duet from *Lakmé* – British Airways
Dvořák: Symphony No. 9 – Hovis Bread
Einaudi: *Le Onde* – John Lewis
Elgar: Cello Concerto – Buxton Natural Mineral Water
Khachaturian: Sabre Dance from *Gayaneh* – Adidas
Orff: 'O fortuna' from *Carmina Burana* – Old Spice
Puccini: 'Nessun dorma' from *Turandot* – Benylin
Rimsky-Korsakov: *Flight of the Bumble Bee* – Lurpak
Tchaikovsky: *Dance of the Reed Flutes* – Cadbury Fruit & Nut
Verdi: Anvil Chorus from *Il Trovatore* – Ragú Pasta Sauce

TEN KIDS' CLASSICS

Bartók – *For Children*
Brahms – *Lullaby*
Britten – *The Young Person's Guide to the Orchestra*
Debussy – *Children's Corner*
Fauré – *Dolly Suite*
Mozart, L – *Toy Symphony*
Poulenc – *The Story of Babar, the Little Elephant*
Prokofieff – *Peter and the Wolf*
Rutter – *Mass of the Children*
Saint-Saëns – *Carnival of the Animals*

★ ★ ★

TEN DONS IN OPERA

Don Alfonso	Donizetti: *Lucrezia Borgia*
Don Alvaro	Verdi: *La forza del destino*
Don Basilio	Rossini: *The Barber of Seville*
Don Carlos	Rameau: *Les indes galantes*
Don Curzio	Mozart: *The Marriage of Figaro*
Don Fernando	Beethoven: *Fidelio*
Don Giovanni	Mozart: *Don Giovanni*
Don José	Bizet: *Carmen*
Don José Martinez	Delius: *Koanga*
Don Quixote	Purcell: *Don Quixote*

NICKNAMES OF TEN OF HAYDN'S SYMPHONIES

Symphony No. 22 in E flat	The Philosopher
Symphony No. 55 in E flat	The Schoolmaster
Symphony No. 60 in C	The Distraught Man
Symphony No. 82 in C	The Bear
Symphony No. 83 in G minor	The Hen
Symphony No. 94 in G major	Surprise
Symphony No. 100 in G	Military
Symphony No. 101 in D	Clock
Symphony No. 103 in E flat	Drumroll
Symphony No. 104 in D	London

CLASSICAL MUSIC USED IN TV THEME TUNES

Horse of the Year Show	Mozart: *A Musical Joke*
The Lone Ranger	Rossini: *William Tell Overture*
Monty Python's Flying Circus	Sousa: *Liberty Bell*
The Onedin Line	Khachaturian: *Adagio of Spartacus and Phrygia*
The Sky at Night	Sibelius: *At the Castle Gate* from *Pelléas et Mélisande*
The South Bank Show	Rachmaninoff: *Variations on a theme of Paganini*
What the Papers Say	Arnold: *English Dance No. 5*

MUSICAL CATALOGUERS

There's only one way to have your name attached to a masterpiece and that's to write one. Isn't it? Well, it is unless you happen to be one of the people who catalogue composers' works. Among them are:

Otto Erich Deutsch – Schubert – (D. numbers)
Anthony van Hoboken – Haydn – (Hob. Numbers)
Ralph Kirkpatrick – Scarlatti – (K. numbers)
Ludwig von Köchel – Mozart – (K. numbers)
Peter Ryom – Vivaldi – (R. numbers)

★ ★ ★

WHEREFORE ART THOU …

These composers have all written music based on William Shakespeare's play *Romeo and Juliet*:

Bellini
Berlioz
Bernstein
Delius
Gounod
Prokofieff
Tchaikovsky

★ ★ ★

COMPOSERS' STAR SIGNS

Aquarius

Delius, Mendelssohn, Mozart

Pisces

Barber, Chopin, Delibes, Handel, Rimsky-Korsakov

Aries

J S Bach, Bartók, Haydn, Rachmaninoff

Taurus

Brahms, Fauré, Prokofieff, Tchaikovsky

Gemini

Elgar, Grieg, Offenbach, Wagner

Cancer

Gluck, Mahler, Orff

Leo

Debussy, Glazounoff

Virgo

Bruckner, Dvořák, Holst, Pachelbel

Libra

Gershwin, Saint-Saëns, Shostakovich, Vaughan Williams

Scorpio

Bizet, Borodin, Britten, Copland, J Strauss Jr

Sagittarius

Beethoven, Berlioz, Donizetti, de Falla

Capricorn

Bruch, Poulenc, Puccini

THIRTY-SOMETHING COMPOSER DEATHS

There has always been a romantic image of the great composer as penniless, ill and dead by the age of 40. Is it true? Well, as for the last bit, there do seem to be a lot of composers who died in their thirties:

Schubert	aged 31
Bellini	aged 33
Mozart	aged 35
Bizet	aged 36
Purcell	aged 36
Gershwin	aged 38
Mendelssohn	aged 38
Chopin	aged 39
Weber	aged 39

MASTERS OF THE KING'S/QUEEN'S MUSIC

1625	Nicholas Lanier
1666	Louis Grabu
1674	Nicholas Staggins
1700	John Eccles
1735	Maurice Green
1755	William Boyce
1779	John Stanley
1786	William Parsons
1817	William Shield
1834	Christian Kramer
1848	George Frideric Handel
1870	William George Cusins
1893	Walter Parratt
1924	Edward Elgar
1934	Walford Davies
1942	Arnold Bax
1953	Arthur Bliss
1975	Malcolm Williamson
2004	Sir Peter Maxwell Davies

★ ★ ★

THREE TENORS CONCERTS

How many Three Tenors concerts do you think there have been? Two? Three maybe? Think again.

Rome	7 July 1990
Monte Carlo	9 June 1994
Los Angeles	16 July 1994
Tokyo	29 June 1996
London	6 July 1996
Vienna	16 July 1996
New York	20 July 1996
Gothenburg	26 July 1996
Munich	23 August 1996
Düsseldorf	24 August 1996
Vancouver	31 December 1996
Toronto	4 January 1997
Melbourne	1 March 1997
Miami	8 March 1997
Modena	17 June 1997
Barcelona	13 July 1997
Paris	10 July 1998
Tokyo	9 January 1999
Pretoria	18 April 1999
Detroit	17 July 1999
San Jose	29 December 1999
Las Vegas	22 April 2000
Washington	7 May 2000
Cleveland	25 June 2000
São Paulo	22 July 2000
Chicago	17 December 2000
Seoul	22 June 2001
Beijing	23 June 2001
Yokohama	27 June 2002
Saint Paul	16 December 2002
Columbus	28 September 2003

CLASSICAL MUSIC USED IN FILMS

Ace Ventura Pet Detective	Mozart: *Eine kleine Nachtmusik*
An American Werewolf in London	Ravel: *Daphnis and Chloé*
Apocalypse Now	Wagner: *Ride of the Valkyries*
As Good As It Gets	Gershwin: *An American in Paris*
Babe	Saint-Saëns: Symphony No. 3
A Beautiful Mind	Mozart: Piano Sonata No. 11
Bend It Like Beckham	Puccini: 'Nessun Dorma' from *Turandot*
Billy Elliott	Tchaikovsky: *Swan Lake*
Brassed Off	Rodrigo: *Concierto de Aranjuez*
Bridget Jones's Diary	Handel: Hallelujah Chorus from *Messiah*
Captain Corelli's Mandolin	Puccini: 'O mio babbino caro' from *Gianni Schicchi*
Catch Me If You Can	Haydn: Piano Concerto No. 11
Chariots of Fire	Allegri: *Miserere*
A Clockwork Orange	Beethoven: Symphony No. 9
The Dead Poets Society	Beethoven: Piano Concerto No. 5
Die Hard	Bach: Brandenburg Concerto No. 3
Driving Miss Daisy	Dvořák: 'Song to the Moon' from *Rusalka*
The Elephant Man	Barber: *Adagio*
The English Patient	Bach: Aria from *Goldberg Variations*
Four Weddings and a Funeral	Handel: *Arrival of the Queen of Sheba*
The French Lieutenant's Woman	Mozart: Piano Sonata No. 15
The Horse Whisperer	Beethoven: Cello Sonata No. 1
Indecent Proposal	Vivaldi: Concerto No. 8 from *L'Estro Armonico*
JFK	Mozart: Horn Concerto No. 2
Johnny English	Handel: *Zadok the Priest*
L A Confidential	Mendelssohn: *Hebrides Overture*
The Ladykillers	Boccherini: *Minuet*
Lara Croft Tomb Raider	Bach: Piano Concerto No. 5 in F minor

Mona Lisa	Puccini: Love Duet from *Madame Butterfly*
Mr Holland's Opus	Beethoven: Symphony No. 7
Mrs Doubtfire	Rossini: 'Largo ...' from *The Barber of Seville*
My Big Fat Greek Wedding	Wagner: Bridal Chorus from *Lohengrin*
My Left Foot	Schubert: '*Trout*' *Quintet*
Natural Born Killers	Orff: *Carmina Burana*
Ocean's Eleven	Debussy: *Clair de lune*
Out of Africa	Mozart: Clarinet Concerto
Philadelphia	Mozart: *Laudate Dominum*
Platoon	Barber: *Adagio for Strings*
Pretty Woman	Vivaldi: *Four Seasons*
A Room with a View	Puccini: Doretta's Dream from *La Rondine*
The Shawshank Redemption	Mozart: 'Che soave zeffiretto' from *The Marriage of Figaro*
The Silence of the Lambs	Bach: *Goldberg Variations*
Sleeping with the Enemy	Berlioz: *Symphonie fantastique*
The talented Mr Ripley	Bach: Italian Concerto
There is something about Mary	Bizet: *Danse bohémienne* from *Carmen Suite No. 2*
Toy Story 2	R Strauss: *Also sprach Zarathustra*
Trainspotting	Bizet: *Habañera* from *Carmen*
The Truman Show	Chopin: Piano Concerto No. 1
Wall Street	Verdi: 'Questa, o quella' from *Rigoletto*
Wayne's World	Tchaikovsky: *Romeo and Juliet*
Who Framed Roger Rabbit	Liszt: *Hungarian Rhapsody No. 2*
2000 Leagues Under The Sea	Bach: Toccata and Fugue in D minor
2001: A Space Odyssey	R Strauss: *Also sprach Zarathustra*

★ ★ ★

COMPOSERS AND THEIR INSTRUMENTS

Bach – organ, violin and keyboard
Berlioz – flute and guitar
Borodin – flute
Britten – viola and piano
Delius – violin
Dvořák – violin, viola and organ
Elgar – organ, violin and piano
Glinka – piano and voice
Grainger – piano
Holst – trombone
Hummel – piano
Johann Strauss Jr – violin and viola
Khachaturian – tuba
Lehar – violin
Lully – guitar, violin and voice
Mozart – viola and piano
Nielsen – trumpet
Offenbach – cello
Respighi – violin and viola
Rossini – piano, viola, horn and voice
Sibelius – violin
Smetana – violin and piano
Suppé – flute
Telemann – violin, zither, oboe and organ
Verdi – organ and piano
Vivaldi – violin
Weber – guitar and piano

GROUPS OF COMPOSERS

Les Six

Milhaud
Tailleferre
Honegger
Durey
Poulenc
Auric

The Mighty Handful

Balakirev
Cui
Borodin
Moussorgsky
Rimsky-Korsakov

The Manchester Group

Peter Maxwell Davies
Harrison Birtwistle
John Ogden
Elgar Haworth

The Second Viennese School

Schoenberg
Webern
Berg

COMPOSERS WHO SHARE BIRTHDAYS

Bruch and Scriabin	6 January
Palestrina and Mendelssohn	3 February
Smetana and Vivaldi	4 March
Telemann and Johann Strauss Sr	14 March
Bach and Moussorgsky	21 March
Busoni and Rachmaninoff	1 April
Brahms and Tchaikovsky	17 April
Massenet and Fauré	12 April
Albinoni and Schumann	8 June
Gounod and Stravinsky	17 June
Pachelbel and Humperdinck	1 September
Bruckner and Milhaud	4 September
Boyce and Arvo Pärt	11 September
Shostakovich and Rameau	25 September
Saint-Saëns and Verdi	9 October
Johann Strauss Jr and Bizet	25 October
Hummel and Copland	14 November
Rodrigo and Britten	22 November

AN A to Z OF LITTLE KNOWN COMPOSERS

Abaelardus
Brod
Cato
Damett
Eechaute
Facoli
Gehot
Hagg
Ishchenko
Jirko
Kaski
Le Flem
Mossi
Nenna
Ostrcil
Pez
Queldryk
Ruffo
Schop
Titov
Uttini
Vitols
Waelput
Xyndas
Youll
Zani

★ ★ ★

COMPOSERS BORN ON SIGNIFICANT DAYS

April Fools' Day	Rachmaninoff
US Independence Day	Daquin
St David's Day	Chopin
Christmas Day	Gibbons
Leap Year Day	Rossini
Bastille Day	Finzi
St Andrew's Day	Alkan

TOP TEN UK SYMPHONY ORCHESTRAS

Bournemouth Symphony Orchestra
City of Birmingham Symphony Orchestra
Hallé Orchestra
London Philharmonic Orchestra
London Symphony Orchestra
Northern Sinfonia
Philharmonia Orchestra
Royal Liverpool Philharmonic Orchestra
Royal Scottish National Orchestra
Ulster Orchestra

THE CLASSIC FM HALL OF FAME

These are the UK's top twenty favourite classical works, as voted by Classic FM listeners:

1   Rachmaninoff: Piano Concerto No. 2 in C minor
2   Vaughan Williams: *The Lark Ascending*
3   Mozart: Clarinet Concerto in A
4   Beethoven: Piano Concerto No. 5 in E flat (*'The Emperor'*)
5   Bruch: Violin Concerto No. 1 in G minor
6   Beethoven: Symphony No. 6 (*'Pastoral'*)
7   Elgar: Cello Concerto in E minor
8   Elgar: *Enigma Variations*
9   Jenkins: *The Armed Man (A Mass for Peace)*
10   Grieg: Piano Concerto in A minor
11   Beethoven: Symphony No. 9 (*'Choral'*)
12   Rachmaninoff: Symphony No. 2 in E minor
13   Vaughan Williams: *Fantasia on a theme by Thomas Tallis*
14   Saint-Saëns: Symphony No. 3 (*'Organ'*)
15   Barber: *Adagio* for strings
16   Sibelius: *Finlandia*
17   Pachelbel: *Canon* in D
18   Bizet: *Pearl Fishers' Duet*
19   Holst: *The Planets Suite*
20   Rachmaninoff: *Rhapsody on a theme of Paganini*

Dinner party trivia

OUT OF THIS WORLD
The first cosmonaut, Yuri Gagarin sang a song called *My Homeland Hears*, written by the great Russian composer Dmitri Shostakovich, over the radio link from his spacecraft back to earth.

PREVIOUS LIVES
Tchaikovsky and Schumann both studied to become lawyers before switching to composing full-time. They weren't alone in opting for a career change: Berlioz trained to be a doctor, Borodin was a scientist, Moussorgsky was a civil servant and Rimsky-Korsakov was in the navy from the age of 12 to 27.

OLDEST ORCHESTRA
According to the Guinness Book of World Records, the very first symphony orchestra was the Gewandhaus Orchestra, which began playing in Leipzig, Germany, in 1743.

THE BORROWERS
Over the years, many great composers have included popular songs in their music. For example, Shostakovich's *Jazz Suites* contain *Tea for Two*, Saint-Saëns borrowed *The Can-Can*, played very slowly to represent the tortoise in the *Carnival of the Animals*, and Walton's *Façade* contains *Oh, I do like to be beside the seaside*.

The converse is also true, with many classical music pieces gaining chart success by being made into pop songs. They include *Since Yesterday* by Strawberry Switchblade (Sibelius's fifth symphony), *Nut Rocker* by Bee Bumble and the

Stingers (Tchaikovsky's *The Nutcracker*), and *Altogether Now* by The Farm (Pachelbel's *Canon in D*).

POP GOES THE CLASSICS

Many musicians who made their fame and fortune through pop or rock music have gone on to compose classical works. These include the former Beatle Sir Paul McCartney, the former Deep Purple keyboard player Jon Lord and the singer/songwriter Billy Joel.

COMPOSERS' NOTES

The most expensive musical manuscript ever to be sold at auction was a collection of Mozart's nine symphonies, which went under the hammer in 1987 for £2.58 million. Six years later, the second most expensive musical score was auctioned off. Its buyer paid £2.13 million for a 575-page manuscript of Beethoven's Symphony No. 9.

MUSICAL MEANING

The word 'philharmonic' is liberally sprinkled throughout the names of many of the world's greatest orchestras. In the UK we have the Royal Philharmonic Orchestra, the Royal Liverpool Philharmonic Orchestra, the London Philharmonic Orchestra and even the Philharmonia Orchestra. But what does the word actually mean? It comes from the two Greek words *phileo* and *harmonikos*. When they're welded together 'philharmonic' translates as 'harmony-loving'.

DISC COUNT

It's claimed that compact discs hold 74 minutes of music to ensure that the whole of Beethoven's Symphony No. 9 could be fitted on one disc without any interruptions.

A BOX OF MOZART

Every year, thousands of people visit Salzburg and literally eat Mozart. Don't worry, cannibalism isn't rife in Austria – Mozart is a brand of chocolate over there. It particularly appeals to visiting tourists.

HER INDOORS

It's no coincidence that Hubert Parry's *Jerusalem* is the calling-card of the Women's Institute. It was adopted following its association with the Votes for Women movement. And the reason why this pressure group adopted the song? Because Parry's wife was herself a suffragette.

TRICK QUESTION

You know those silly questions: 'Who wrote Beethoven's Fifth?' or: 'Which country's official song is the French National Anthem?' Well, just be careful if someone asks you 'Who wrote the overture to Offenbach's *Orpheus in the Underworld*?' Because it was actually added later by Carl Binder.

PUBLISH AND BE GRAND!

It's a little-known fact that Boosey & Hawkes, publisher not only of this book you are reading but also of many of the world's greatest composers – Rachmaninoff, Stravinsky, Prokofieff and many more – actually started life as a general lending library. John Boosey set it up in the City of London between 1765 and 1770. It wasn't until more than 150 years later in 1930 that Boosey met his Hawkes. William Henry Hawkes had been a respected band musician, and the two names have been making sweet music together ever since.

BOGEY AT THE 18th

It's said that Kenneth J Alford got the idea for the tune *Colonel Bogey* while on the golf course. When his golf partner teed off, he would always whistle two notes to warn anyone on the fairway. The notes stuck in his head, all the way round, and became the first two notes of the now world-famous tune.

FIVE LINES THAT CHANGED THE WORLD

One of the great unsung heroes of classical music – in fact, all music – is Guido d'Arezzo. He was the clever chap who came up with the five lines on which almost all music is now written, called a 'stave'. He thought of it at more or less the same time as somebody in China invented gunpowder.

FOOTBALL SCORES

The Montagues and Capulets from Prokofieff's ballet *Romeo and Juliet* accompanies Sunderland footballers on to the pitch each week at home games.

SIGN LANGUAGE

You know those house signs that you occasionally see which are an amalgamation of the names of the couple living inside? So, 'Marron', for example, probably means that Margaret and Ron live there. Well, genius though he was, Rachmaninoff was not above doing it, too. His house on the edge of Lake Lucerne was called 'Senar', which was short for **SE**rge and **NA**talya **R**achmaninoff.

CHANGING THE HILDEGARD

Hildegard of Bingen, one of the foremost early composers, not to mention one of the very few famous women composers, wasn't born in Bingen. Nor did she live or die in Bingen. She was actually from Rupertsberg, just down the road. Maybe Bingen rolled off the tongue easier.

SYMPHONIC VARIATION

Mozart wrote 41 symphonies but you could go to Jupiter and back before you find his symphony no. 37. It doesn't actually exist. The symphony that was erroneously labelled Mozart's symphony no. 37 was actually composed by someone else. Mozart had copied it out for his friend. Of course, if you ever see a manuscript of it in a junkshop, snap it up anyway!

LIVE AT ABBEY ROAD

When Abbey Road Studios opened in London in 1931, the first recording ever made there was of Elgar's *Falstaff*, with the composer himself conducting. There's no photo of him walking over the zebra crossing outside, though.

LISTEN EAR

Allegri's glorious *Miserere* was written for the Sistine Chapel Choir in Rome. The Pope declared the music to be so powerful that the score was closely guarded in case other tried to copy the music. It's said that when the young Wolfgang Amadeus Mozart heard the *Miserere* performed during a visit to the chapel, he rushed home and wrote it out in full from memory.

FINALES

Anton Webern is just one composer who met a rather sad, unfortunate end. He was shot by an American soldier after a misunderstanding over language. Then there was Jean-Baptiste Lully, who hit himself in the toe with a conducting stick, and died from the wound.

SOUNDS FAMILIAR

Classical composers aren't averse to reusing a story that someone else has told before. Take the mythological tale of Orpheus, for instance. Monteverdi used it for his opera *L'Orfeo* in 1607. Gluck wrote a new version in Italian in 1762 and in French in 1774. Then Offenbach told the story all over again in 1858 in his opera *Orpheus in the Underworld*.

YOU CAN'T BE GOOD AT EVERYTHING

Albert Einstein was the man who formulated the theory of relativity, who revolutionised our grasp of matters space and time, who even tweaked the Brownian theory of motion. He was also a keen amateur violinist. Once, below the window of his Mercer Street apartment in Princeton, his violin teacher was heard to say, 'Oh for goodness sake, Albert, can't you count?'

WHOSE HOUSE?

A house in Brook Street, London, just along the road from Claridges, was home to two musical superstars from different eras. Both the classical composer George Frideric Handel and the rock guitarist Jimi Hendrix lived in the same central London pad – although they were resident there a good 200 years apart.

SLOWLY DECOMPOSING

After they died, it took a while for many of the greatest composers to be allowed to rest in peace. Bach, Mozart, Haydn, Beethoven and Scubert were all exhumed and reburied at various times. Mozart, Haydn and Donizetti's skulls were also parted from their bodies when they were buried. There seems to have been a roaring trade in Haydn skulls – with several doing the rounds in the years after his death.

PARALLEL LIVES

Bach and Handel were both born in the same year – 1685. Both suffered from cataracts and were treated, unsuccessfully, by the same British optician.

KILLED IN ACTION

The life of the composer George Butterworth, best known for his quintessentially English piece *On the Banks of Green Willow*, was tragically cut short when he was killed fighting for his country in the Battle of the Somme.

THE NAME GAME

Stanley Myers' *Cavatina* is often known as 'the theme from *The Deer Hunter*'. But things could have been different. It would be fair also to call it 'the theme from *The Walking Stick*'. Myers originally wrote it for the 1971 film called *The Walking Stick* and simply reused it seven years later in *The Deer Hunter*.

TONIGHT, ON SOLO VACUUM CLEANER …

What do composers do when they run out of conventional instruments for which they want to compose? Well, often they start to include all manner of weird and wonderful new 'instruments' in their scores. Gershwin put car horns in *An American in Paris*, Luciano Berio included a part for car springs, while the composer of silence, John Cage, once wrote a piece for liquidiser. And Malcolm Arnold really did write a piece for vacuum cleaner. Three vacuum cleaners in fact. Together with a floor polisher and four rifles.

TAKING IT ON THE CHIN

The German composer Louis Spohr was a bit of a revolutionary on the quiet. As well as being one of the first conductors to use a baton to keep time, he also invented the chin rest for the violin, sometime around 1820.

EINE KLEINE COOL MUSIK
When Mozart came to London on tour, he stayed at 20 Frith Street, lodging with one Thomas Williamson. There's a plaque on the wall of the house and, today, fans of a different kind of music stand and stare at it – it's directly opposite Ronnie Scott's Jazz Club.

ANAGRAMS
An anagram of 'Gustav Mahler' is 'M Ravel's a thug' and if you jumble up the letters in 'Robert Schumann', you arrive at 'Brahms Nocturne'.

YOUNG TALENT
Some of the greatest classical composers didn't hang around when it came to making music in public. The Spanish composer Isaac Albeniz had his first professional engagement at just four years old. Felix Mendelssohn was nine years old when he first appeared before an audience. Wolfgang Amadeus Mozart was six when he went on his first tour, way ahead of César Franck – he didn't go on the road for the first time until the relatively advanced age of eleven.

HITTING THE HIGH NOTES
When you hear Mozart's beautiful soprano motet *Exultate jubilate*, does it make your eyes water? It could be because it was originally written not for a soprano at all, but for the castrato Venanzio Rauzzini.

RECORD BREAKER
The biggest-selling classical CD of all time is The Three Tenors Live in Concert, which was recorded live in Rome in 1990.

Classical quotes

Talking about music will never be a substitute for performing or listening to it, but many of classical music's greatest practitioners have had a thing or two to say about their art – along with that of their colleagues.

We've arranged the quotes into sections dealing with composers, conductors and musicians. Singers, of course, make up a separate section.

In addition, insults get a section of their own (after all, classical musicians have such a large repertoire of them), as do some of the many barbs directed towards one composer in particular – Wagner.

Musical theories

The story probably went something like this: first came the wheel. Then came the cart. A few moments after that came the backseat driver, who proceeded to commentate from the back of the cart.

From time immemorial, the moment anything vaguely significant happened, there appears to have been someone on hand to theorise, posit and hypothesise.

Here are just a few examples of what some people thought it was all about. 'It' being music, of course.

I don't know much about classical music. For years I thought *Goldberg Variations* were something Mr and Mrs Goldberg tried on their wedding night.

    – Woody Allen, film actor and director, *Stardust Memories* (1980)

Music hath charms to soothe the savage beast, but I'd try a revolver first.

    – John Billings, humorist.

Learning music by reading about it is like making love by mail.

    – Isaac Stern, violinist.

Even Bach comes down to the basic suck, blow, suck, suck, blow.

    – Larry Adler, harmonica player.

Music with dinner is an insult both to the cook and the violinist.

    – G K Chesterton, writer.

Creativity is more than just being different. Anybody can play weird – that's easy. What's hard is to be as simple as Bach. Making the simple awesomely simple, that's creativity.

– Charles Mingus, composer.

Definition of a true musician: one who, when he hears a lady singing in the bathtub, he puts his ear to the keyhole.

– Morey Amsterdam, actor and comedian.

There's only two ways to sum up music: either it's good or it's bad. If it's good you don't mess about it – you just enjoy it.

– Louis Armstrong, trumpet player.

[Music] can be made anywhere, is invisible, and does not smell.

– W H Auden, poet, *In Praise of Limestone* (1951).

Too many pieces of music finish too long after the end.

– Igor Stravinsky, composer.

I occasionally play works by contemporary composers, and for two reasons. First, to discourage the composer from writing any more, and secondly to remind myself how much I appreciate Beethoven.

– Jascha Heifetz, violinist

About contemporary music:
Three farts and a raspberry, orchestrated.

– Sir John Barbirolli, conductor.

Modern music is as dangerous as cocaine.

– Pietro Mascagni, composer.

Music helps not the toothache.

– George Herbert, poet.

★ ★ ★

Why should the devil have all the good tunes?

> – Rowland Hill, inventor of the 'Penny Black' stamp.

I believe in Bach, the Father, Beethoven, the Son, and Brahms, the Holy Ghost of music.

> – Hans von Bülow, conductor and pianist.

For changing people's manners and altering their customs there is nothing better than music.

> – Shu Ching, 600 BC

[Music] is the only sensual pleasure without vice.

> – Samuel Johnson, lexicographer.

Military justice is to justice what military music is to music.

> – Groucho Marx, actor and writer.

Truly there would be reason to go mad if it were not for music.

> – Peter Ilyich Tchaikovsky, composer.

To listen is an effort, and just to hear is no merit. A duck hears also.

> – Igor Stravinsky, composer.

One should try everything once, except incest and folk-dancing.

> – Arnold Bax, composer.

Musicians. Funny bunch. Granted, in many ways they've given us some of life's sweetest moments. But ask virtually any of them what they think of their colleagues and, well, sweet almost always turns to sour. Sometimes they comment on the works, but mostly, they comment on the people. Well, why beat about the bush? As they say in the circus – go for the juggler!

So here is a whole section devoted to the musical 'put-down'.

You have Van Gogh's ear for music.

> – Billy Wilder, film director and writer.

Rossini would have been a great composer if his teacher had spanked him enough on the backside.

> – Ludwig van Beethoven, composer.

I played over the music of that scoundrel Brahms. What a giftless bastard! It annoys me that this self-inflated mediocrity is hailed as genius.

> – Peter Ilyich Tchaikovsky, composer.

On Hector Berlioz's *Symphonie Fantastique*:
What a good thing this isn't music.

> – Gioachino Rossini, composer.

Also about Hector Berlioz:
One ought to wash one's hands after dealing with one of his scores.

> – Felix Mendelssohn, composer.

I'm told that Saint-Saëns has informed a delighted public that since the war began he has composed music for the stage, melodies, an elegy and a piece for the trombone. If he'd been making shell-cases instead it might have been all the better for music.

> – Maurice Ravel, composer, who himself worked as an ambulance driver during the First World War.

Obituary of Jacques Offenbach, the man who composed the *Can-Can*:
He has written nothing that will live, nothing that will make the world better. His name as well as his music will soon be forgotten.

> – *Chicago Tribune.*

About Claude Debussy's *La Mer*:
The audience ... expected the ocean, something big, something colossal, but they were served instead with some agitated water in a saucer.

> – Louis Schneider, composer.

Debussy is like a painter who looks at his canvas to see what more he can take out. Strauss is like a painter who has covered every inch and then takes the paint he has left and throws it at the canvas.

> – Ernest Bloch, composer.

Listening to the fifth symphony of Ralph Vaughan Williams is like staring at a cow for 45 minutes.

> – Aaron Copland, composer.

About the composer, Nikolai Rimsky-Korsakov:
What a name! It suggests fierce whiskers stained with vodka!

> – *The Musical Courier.*

At the premiere of Mozart's opera *The Marriage of Figaro*:
Far too noisy, my dear Mozart. Far too many notes.

> – Emperor Joseph II.

To a violinist who believed that a passage was impossible to play:
When I composed that, I was conscious of being inspired by God Almighty. Do you think I consider your puny little fiddle when He speaks to me?
— Ludwig van Beethoven, composer.

On his way out of a party:
If there is anyone here whom I have not insulted, I beg his pardon.
— Johannes Brahms, composer.

Compose yourself

Now this is a revealing section: composers, and what they said about the art of composing. Suprisingly, there's very little of the luvvie in here. Instead, on the whole, the great composers seemed to have two feet very much on the ground.

Read on and you'll find out why Mozart identified with female pigs and what could be called the Rossini Doorstep Challenge – although, as far as we can tell, there is no hard evidence to suggest that Rossini ever took in washing.

It is clear that the first specification for a composer is to be dead.
> – Arthur Honegger, composer, in *I am a Composer* (1951)

We're not worried about writing for posterity. We just want it to sound good right now.
> – Duke Ellington, composer.

Composers shouldn't think too much – it interferes with their plagiarism.
> – Howard Dietz, songwriter.

A good composer does not imitate; he steals.
> – Igor Stravinsky, composer.

Since Mozart's day, composers have learnt the art of making music throatily and palpitatingly sexual.
> – Aldous Huxley, writer.

I write as a sow piddles.
> – Wolfgang Amadeus Mozart, composer.

It is sobering to consider that when Mozart was my age, he had already been dead for a year.
> – Tom Lehrer, satirist.

The old idea ... of a composer suddenly having a terrific idea and sitting up all night to write it is nonsense. Night time is for sleeping.

– Benjamin Britten, composer.

Composing is like driving down a foggy road toward a house. Slowly, you see more details of the house – the colour of the slates and bricks, the shape of the windows. The notes are the bricks and mortar of the house.

– Benjamin Britten, composer.

In order to compose, all you have to do is remember a tune that nobody else thought of.

– Robert Schumann, composer.

Never compose anything unless not composing it becomes a positive nuisance to you.

– Gustav Holst, composer.

It is not hard to compose, but it is wonderfully hard to let the superfluous notes fall under the table.

– Johannes Brahms, composer.

Give me a laundry list and I will set it to music.

– Gioachino Rossini, composer.

Every composer knows the anguish and despair occasioned by forgetting ideas which one has no time to write down.

– Hector Berlioz, composer.

Composers tend to assume that everyone loves music. Surprisingly enough, everyone doesn't.

– Aaron Copland, composer.

Pay no attention to what the critics say. No statue has ever been put up to a critic.

– Jean Sibelius, composer.

On hearing John Cage's *4′33″*, which comprises no music, just four and a half minutes of silence:
I look forward to hearing his longer works.

– Igor Stravinsky, composer.

Having adapted Beethoven's sixth symphony for *Fantasia*, Walt Disney commented: 'Gee! That'll make Beethoven.'

– Marshall McLuhan, media commentator, in *Culture is our Business* (1970)

Beethoven and Liszt have contributed to the advent of long hair.

– Louis Moreau Gottschalk, pianist, composer and conductor.

Imagine this: all of the composers have met up in the afterlife and a roll-call is being taken of their names. When it comes to Wagner, it turns out that he's the only one who's insisted on a separate room.

He merits his own section not because we think he is the greatest, but because whenever musicians were looking for a target, more of them set their sights on 'Little Richard' than any other. Perhaps his mother should have taught her somewhat vertically challenged son that size isn't everything.

I can't listen to too much Wagner. I start to get the urge to conquer Poland.
  – Woody Allen, film director and writer, *Manhattan Murder Mystery* (1993)

I've been told that Wagner's music is better than it sounds.
– Mark Twain, writer.

Wagner has lovely moments but awful quarters of an hour.
– Gioachino Rossini, composer.

I love Wagner, but the music I prefer is that of a cat hung up by its tail outside a window and trying to stick to the panes of glass with its claws.
– Charles Baudelaire, poet.

I like Wagner's music better than any other music. It is so loud that one can talk the whole time without people hearing what one says. That is a great advantage.
– Oscar Wilde, writer, *The Picture of Dorian Gray* (1981)

One can't judge Wagner's opera *Lohengrin* after a first hearing, and I certainly don't intend hearing it a second time.
– Gioachino Rossini, composer.

Passing the baton

It's easy to feel sorry for football managers. When all goes well, the team gets the credit. When all goes badly, it's their fault and they're out.

Conductors are a bit like football managers, only in reverse. When everything goes well in a concert, they are portrayed as demigods, for managing to make seventy people play with one voice. When it goes badly, well, they didn't have a chance with those musicians, did they?

Cue a 'baton charge' of venom-fuelled quotes, usually aimed at the orchestra.

There are two golden rules for an orchestra: start together and finish together: The public doesn't give a damn what goes on in between.

– Sir Thomas Beecham, conductor.

I am not interested in having an orchestra sound like itself. I want it to sound like the composer.

– Leonard Bernstein, conductor and composer.

Said to a member of an orchestra:
God tells me how the music should sound, but you stand in the way!

– Arturo Toscanini, conductor.

You can chase a Beethoven symphony all your life and not catch up.

– André Previn, conductor and composer.

A good conductor ought to be a good chauffeur. The qualities that make the one also make the other. They are concentration, an incessant control of attention, and presence of mind – the conductor only has to add a little sense of music.

– Serge Rachmaninoff, composer.

To members of his orchestra, who were not performing well:
After I die I shall return to earth as the doorkeeper of a bordello, and I won't let one of you in.

– Arturo Toscanini, conductor.

If anyone has conducted a Beethoven performance, and then doesn't have to go to an osteopath, then there's something wrong.

– Sir Simon Rattle, conductor.

You know why conductors live so long? Because we perspire so much.

– Sir John Barbirolli, conductor.

Don't perspire while conducting – only the audience should get warm.

– Richard Strauss, composer and conductor.

The conductor has the advantage of not seeing the audience.

– André Kostelanetz, conductor.

Said to a female cellist:
Madam, you have between your legs an instrument capable of giving pleasure to thousands – and all you can do is scratch it.

– Sir Thomas Beecham. Also attributed to
fellow conductor, Arturo Toscanini.

Harpists spend 90 per cent of their lives tuning their harps and 10 per cent playing out of tune.

– Igor Stravinsky, composer.

Never look at the trombones, it only encourages them.

– Richard Strauss, composer and conductor.

The tuba is certainly the most intestinal of instruments – the very lower bowel of music.

– Peter de Vries, writer, *The Glory of the Hummingbird* (1974).

Have you ever met someone famous and been a little disappointed because you found out that they were smaller than you thought, or that they looked older in real life?

Well, a similar thing can happen when you ask yourself the question 'I wonder what's going through the musician's head when they are playing Chopin, conducting their own music, or singing at La Scala?' Some of these questions are answered in this section, along with the odd tip on how to be a performer. You might find that you wish you'd never asked.

I know two kinds of audience only – one coughing and one not coughing.

> – Artur Schnabel, pianist.

I'm a flute player, not a flautist. I don't have a flaut and I've never flauted.

> – James Galway, flute player.

I never understood the need for a 'live' audience. My music, because of its extreme quietude, would be happiest with a dead one.

> – Igor Stravinsky, composer.

Making music is like making love: the act is always the same, but each time is different.

> – Artur Rubinstein, pianist.

Advice from one pianist to another:
When a piece gets difficult, make faces.

> – Artur Schnabel, pianist.

The notes I handle no better than many pianists. But the pauses between the notes – ah, that is where the art resides.

– Artur Schnabel, pianist.

It's easy to play any musical instrument: all you have to do is touch the right key at the right time and the instrument will play itself.

– Johann Sebastian Bach, composer.

You don't need any brains to listen to music.

– Luciano Pavarotti, tenor.

After playing Chopin, I feel as if I had been weeping over sins that I had never committed.

– Oscar Wilde, writer.

The music teacher came twice a week to bridge the awful gap between Dorothy and Chopin.

– George Ade, humorist.

Mine was the kind of piece in which nobody knew what was going on – including the composer, the conductor and the critics. Consequently I got pretty good critics.

– Oscar Levant, pianist and composer, in *A Smattering of Ignorance* (1940)

I'm not handsome, but when women hear me play, they come crawling to my feet.

– Nicolò Paganini, violinist and composer.

I cannot tell you how much I love to play for people. Would you believe it – sometimes when I sit down to practise and there is no one else in the room, I have to stifle an impulse to ring for the elevator man and offer him money to come and hear me.

– Artur Rubinstein, pianist.

[Musicians] talk of nothing but money and jobs. Give me businessmen every time. They really are interested in music and art.

– Jean Sibelius, composer.

Last night the band played Beethoven. Beethoven lost.

– Anon.

Why does opera have its own quotes section? To answer that, you have to understand that the opera world has a reputation for being a little inward-looking, shall we say.

It is no coincidence that the phrase 'prima donna' has come to be associated with bad behaviour. As the legend goes, a singer will be the one at a party saying, 'But less of this talk about *me*. Let's talk about *you* – what do *you* think about me?'

Is it true? Judge for yourself.

How wonderful the opera world would be if there were no singers.

– Gioachino Rossini, composer.

Singers have the most marvellous breath control and can kiss for about ten minutes.

– Jilly Cooper, novelist.

Opera's when a guy gets stabbed in the back and instead of bleeding he sings.

– Ed Gardner, American radio personality.

About Wagner's opera *Parsifal*:
The kind of opera that starts at six o'clock and after it has been going three hours you look at your watch and it says 6.20.

– David Randolph, conductor.

A review of Verdi's opera *Rigoletto*, shortly after its premiere:
Rigoletto lacks melody. This opera has hardly any chance of being kept in the repertoire.

– *Gazette musicale de Paris*.

I don't mind what language an opera is sung in so long as it is a language I don't understand.

– Sir Edward Appleton, physicist.

If you think you've hit a false note, sing loud. When in doubt, sing loud.

– Robert Merrill, baritone.

I cannot switch my voice. My voice is not like an elevator going up and down.

– Maria Callas, soprano.

About a soprano:
If she can strike a low G or F like a death-rattle and high F like the shriek of a little dog when you step on its tail, the house will resound with acclamations.

– Hector Berlioz, composer.

No good opera plot can be sensible, for people do not sing when they are feeling sensible.

– W H Auden, poet.

After hearing an opera by another composer:
I like your opera – I think I will set it to music.

– Ludwig van Beethoven, composer.

AND FINALLY …

Most people wouldn't know music if it came up and bit them on the ass.

– Frank Zappa, composer.

Index of composers

NOTES

These pages are for you to make your own notes on
things that you need to remember about music –
why not make your own ephemera more permanent?

NOTES

These pages are for you to make your own notes on
things that you need to remember about music –
why not make your own ephemera more permanent?

NOTES

These pages are for you to make your own notes on
things that you need to remember about music –
why not make your own ephemera more permanent?